Taking A Chance on God

Exploring God's Presence in our Lives

Taking A Chance on God

Exploring God's Presence in our Lives

Reverend Bobbie McKay, Ph.D.
and Lewis A. Musil, MFA

iUniverse, Inc.
New York Lincoln Shanghai

Taking A Chance on God
Exploring God's Presence in our Lives

iUniverse books may be ordered through booksellers or by contacting:

iUniverse
2021 Pine Lake Road, Suite 100
Lincoln, NE 68512
www.iuniverse.com
1-800-Authors (1-800-288-4677)

ISBN: 978-0-595-46097-7 (pbk)
ISBN: 978-0-595-91752-5 (cloth)
ISBN: 978-0-595-90397-9 (ebk)

Printed in the United States of America

This book is dedicated to
George Gallup Jr., Lester Knight,
and the Reverend Doctor Gil Bowen,
special friends and Gifts from God,
whose faith in God and in the Mission God gave us
have made this book possible.

With love and gratitude,
Bobbie and Lew

Contents

Forward: George Gallup Jr.

Open your spiritual eyes and say "yes" to God is the passionate and persistent message of this remarkable book. Readers are urged to step aside from their frantic day-to-day existence and recognize the unexpected presence and action of God in their lives.

The authors, Bobbie McKay and Lew Musil, are understandably enthusiastic about conveying this message to readers because they, themselves, have traveled extensively across the country, listening to the heart-gripping and trans-formative spiritual experiences of hundreds of people in all walks of life.

These case histories (and more than 3000 people were interviewed for this study, which is the basis for this book) are so powerful and compelling that the authors say that they themselves have been transformed by the process. "It was an indescribably unexpected journey," they write, "filled with 3000 surprises and utterly life-changing for us."

TAKING A CHANCE ON GOD is an important, breakthrough book because not only is it based on a huge number of in-depth and personal stories of God's action in human life, but because these interviews form a representative sample (with the correct proportions of various religious and demographic groups) and can thus be projected to the nation as a whole. The study and book fully satisfy the need for both professionally conducted qualitative and quantitative research. The authors have approached this exploration of God's interaction with humans with full objectivity, not imposing any theological or programmatic restrictions on the questions for findings. Their writing represents a clear and lively portrait of the baseline dimensions of spirituality of the U.S. population.

Most of the people they interviewed were ready and eager to share their experiences. "The unexpected and transforming presence of God," the authors write, "is occurring at the present time and is happening to ordinary people." Indeed, readers will find themselves in some of the transforming and liberating experiences recorded.

McKay and Musil have poured their hearts, and minds and souls into this effort. They have a treasure in their hands, and their enthusiasm about the project was apparent when we met together on two occasions at my offices in Princeton, New Jersey, in which we discussed the survey results from the nine-page questionnaire, and their implications for individuals and society as a whole.

Nine of every ten persons interviewed reported having had at least one experience of spiritual healing that had transformed their lives. The statistical evidence clearly indicates that spiritual healings happen all the time, and to all sorts and conditions of people. The survey data and their own personal experience from a multitude of face-to-face interviews lead the authors to point to a "healing reality in a broken world," and to state boldly, "The question of the existence of God is not a matter of faith, but of statistical reality."

McKay and Musil remind us that the unfilled moment or split second becomes an opportunity to see God. We are to continue to be present and available to God. When we walk with God, we shall not simply believe, but know. This book is an earnest invitation to readers to say "yes" to God, to be quick to obey spiritual promptings and leadings, and to ask the critical question: Where is God in this moment?

In a concluding chapter, "Taking a Chance on God", McKay and Musil offer practical suggestions for entering the nearer presence of God: assume God is present and active, and even if you do not believe this, act as if this is true. Don't look for God in the usual places, and keep your heart and mind open—and look for surprises.

Analysis of the findings uncovers certain basic themes in the responses of persons who have had a trans-formative healing experience: they are less self-centered and ego-bound; more open to other people; and have a greater sense of peace in their lives. Having received the gift of God's presence, say these two intrepid explorers of the inner life, McKay and Musil, one is under obligation to share it. Not to share the gift is to lose it. Healing stories will heal others.

It is exciting to reflect upon the potential that this imposing body of qualitative and quantitative research has for bringing about healing relationships among people at the deepest level. The authors have done the scientific and religious worlds a great service in probing beneath the surface of life to give us new and fresh insight into the action and presence of God in human existence.

Introduction:
The Search For Spiritual Healing

Thirteen years ago, we initiated what was supposed to be a small study on the meaning of spiritual healing in mainstream Protestantism, which turned into a landmark, international study of the spiritual experiences of over three thousand people in Protestant, Catholic and Reform Jewish Congregations. The surprising results of that study formed the basis for this book and are critically important in our understanding of spiritual life in mainstream America.

A lot of books have been written about spiritual matters. If you've bought such books or are browsing this one you probably have a collection of them yourself. But this one is different from the others you may have read. This book is not based on theory, theology, creed or pop psycho-spirituality. It is based on an interfaith study of over three thousand people, selected to represent ethnic, socioeconomic, and geographic diversity, who have had transforming experiences with the presence or action of God in their lives. It encompasses not only their stories and their words, but includes the results of a nine page questionnaire about their experiences. We believe their stories can point your life toward the same transformed state.

This is not a "how to" book, but it is a book of the possibility of God present and active in your life which can transform you. It can give you the guidelines of this experience which we have derived from our study population and predispose you to be open to God's transforming presence which is always available, if not always seen.

This is not a "religious" book. It is not based on creedal organization or theology. Rather it reflects the experiences of people which, while individual, were unexpectedly universal in nature. While we drew our population from religious congregations, it turned out we simply found people with transforming spiritual stories who happened to gather with us in a church/synagogue building. What they told us was not the product of their institutional affiliation or even their creedal religious system, but what they discovered about God in their ordinary, every day life.

This is not a book in which you can "get God", but it may well be a book that will allow God to get you, if you remain open to the possibility. What this book is really about is recognizing God's transforming presence in your life and opening your "spiritual eyes" to that reality.

So, come along as we tell you of our amazing journey, what we found and most important what it can mean for you. But as you walk with us, put aside the press of the information age in which instant gratification isn't soon enough and take an easy stroll through the spiritual wonders that are always present in this life, but so rarely seen.

Give yourself a break and step out of time into the timelessness of the Spirit. And don't be concerned with how long it takes to get to the end of the path. Walking the path itself is a holy task. As one of the people in our study remarked, "God works on God's own time, but God is never late!"

But be forewarned! When your spiritual eyes are opened, you may find your life changing beyond your wildest imaginings.

What we didn't mention is that God's other name is … **"SURPRISE!"**

PART I
Receiving The Gift.

1

Finding The Quest In A Question

We never set out to do a research study. We were only looking for the answer to a few questions about spiritual healing. It's not that we were ignorant about research. But it was not part of *our* life planning to do an elaborate research project.

However, nearly forty-three years ago, Bobbie had a profound spiritual experience which transformed her life from being an "ordinary housewife" to unexpectedly becoming an ordained minister, licensed clinical psychologist, author and public speaker. Thirteen years ago, she caught her breath, stopped and asked an unforgettable question. *"Have other people had the same kind of experience that I had, which turned my life upside down and set me on a brand new spiritual course of life?"*

She described her experience as a "spiritual healing" because her spirit felt healed and her life absolutely changed: a kind of spiritual course correction that was unexpected, life giving and permanent. Thus the journey to answer her question was begun and the "Spiritual Healing Project" was born. We became unexpected researchers entering remarkably unfamiliar territory marked by an endless number of surprises!

Now most research studies follow a typical pattern: they begin with a question, followed by a series of hypotheses to be proved or disproved in relation to the question. They conduct a review of what others have already said about the question; and usually include some kind of hunch about the outcome. With a few hundred subjects completing whatever test instrument has been designed or selected one of the hypotheses *may* answer the question.

But we were on an entirely different track. We began with a question, but didn't follow it with any hypotheses to be proved. We thought we'd find a small sample of churches to participate in our study. What we were given was a chance to interview more than three thousand people from over one hundred fifty religious communities.

We didn't look at what other researchers had said. Instead, we listened to over one thousand stories from our participants which provided us with an unexpected but remarkably cohesive base of knowledge. In point of fact, we were simply open to whatever was to come in answer to our basic question.

Now questions and answers are part of the rhythm of life and not just the purview of research studies. They underlie our daily life in such a constant way that we become as unaware of them as we do of breathing. Questions tug at us, however, whether they are trivial (what will I wear today?) or fundamental (what's it all really about?). And they drive us to seek answers.

But not all questions are created equal. Sometimes, there is a question which surpasses our syntax and gainsays our grammar and leads us into distant lands. That is particularly true of spiritual questions. Spiritual questions are distinguished by being other centered. Their compass always points to that which we call GOD, whatever meaning you put to those three letters. That indefinable word is the lodestar of spiritual seeking and those questions are oriented to a different north.

Bobbie asked a deceptively simple question which didn't necessarily look like a "spiritual" question. But it turned out to be the question that would transform our spiritual lives and it taught us that sometimes the only way to answer a spiritual question is to tell a story. So this book is the story of our spiritual journey, entirely directed by the ongoing presence of God in our lives.

At first, we wondered if the words, "spiritual healing" would be words to which others could respond. They're not commonly used in mainstream religious congregations and frankly are pretty "loaded" with misconceptions and misunderstandings. Would we be stopped at the very beginning of our journey by using language that could turn people away from our study before it was even started? The answer was simple, "Let's find out."

The place we chose to start our inquiry was the United Church of Christ, the denomination to which Bobbie is connected and a natural choice in terms of subjects for our study. It is an amalgamation of liberal and conservative Christians, centered in the mainstream, geographically dispersed, socioeconomically representative and with a marvelously diverse ethnic representation.

The method that God supplied was simplicity itself. Visit fifteen or twenty diverse congregations and ask two questions: (1) What words do you use to describe/define the phrase "spiritual healing"; and (2) What stories do you tell about "spiritual healing" that fit your description/definition? That seemed to be the most direct approach to answering Bobbie's question of whether others had a similar experience to hers.

We had no idea what we would find, but hoped there would be someone(s) who could answer our questions. We were not influenced by previous literature on spiritual healing because we didn't look for it. We had nothing to prove or disprove which meant that the data we would collect would not have to be forced into a preconceived direction. We simply asked two key questions. The rest was up to the people we interviewed and God. Indeed the concern was more would we find any consistent answers at all?

Our official journey began in Cleveland, where the United Church of Christ (UCC) has its headquarters, to seek permission to contact churches in the denomination with our study. We met with the appropriate hierarchy, told them of our plan to visit a representative sample of fifteen or twenty churches and ask two questions about spiritual healing to any members of the congregation who chose to attend our meeting. They listened politely and then asked an unexpected question: "Why would you want to do that? No one is interested in the subject of spiritual healing in the United Church of Christ!" As much as we loved questions, this one was definitely not on our list.

We thought for a moment and then Bobbie said the magic words which are the open sesame to all corporate and institutional bodies. "We're not asking for any money. We'll pay for this ourselves. We just want your endorsement of this project." The "price" was exactly right and endorsement followed. But we were advised to invite a whole lot of churches to participate because the turndown rate was bound to be very high.

Returning home we discovered to our surprise and consternation that we had sixty one hundred churches from which to choose our sample. One year later, after considerable anguish and persistence, we possessed a wonderful sample of one hundred congregations which met all our criteria of ethnic, socioeconomic, geographic and preference diversity, including representation from urban, rural, suburban, large church, small church, successful church, dying church, multi staff, single pastor churches. It was an amazing tapestry of the different faces of the denomination.

We drafted a letter to our one hundred churches explaining we would like to meet with anyone interested in the subject of spiritual healing. It was not necessary to have had such an experience nor to talk about it at the meeting. We stressed we were not spiritual healers ourselves, did not do spiritual healing nor were we experts on the subject. We were simply researchers trying to understand the meaning of these words by asking people for words and stories of their own experiences with spiritual healing.

We also asked them to fill out an anonymous nine page questionnaire we had written to help us obtain more data and to give people who don't like to talk in public a private way to share. The whole process would take a couple of hours.

The letters were written, addressed and sent on their way. We had no idea what would happen. If the powers that be in the United Church of Christ were right, it would be damn little. We waited.

In two weeks, we received ninety-six "yes" answers to our letters. Two weeks later we added four more churches giving us a sample of an even one hundred churches in the study. We had found our quest and our numbers exceeded anything we could have imagined or sought.

But elation was quickly alloyed with the remembrance we had agreed to pay for this study ourselves. It seemed simple enough to find funds to visit fifteen or twenty churches. But one hundred churches? That was a different matter altogether. And yet, there really was no choice. If this was the gift God had given us, who were we to say anything but "yes" ourselves.

Planning the logistics of the project presented a few problems aside from the financial ones. Bobbie was engaged in a full time private practice as a clinical psychologist as well as being a pastor to a small church community. Lew had his own business and we had nine grandchildren to take up our "spare" time. At the most, we had weekends or possibly a day or two around the weekend to conduct the study. The planning it took to get various congregations lined up within those parameters made the Normandy invasion seem like directions to the church picnic.

On April 19th, 1996, we met with our first congregation, an African American Church in Chicago. Twenty five people gathered to hear what this was all about and within a few moments were sharing remarkable words and stories of the Presence and Action of God in their lives. Three thousand people and seven years later, we paused to catch our breath.

In those seven years, we had grown from a two question project to an interfaith, international study of Protestant (UCC and Episcopal), Catholic and Reform Jewish congregations. We would conduct a second study on spiritual life over the age of sixty. We had traveled to Oxford University in England to present our study to the Alister Hardy Religious Experience Research Centre, an organization devoted to collecting stories of spiritual experiences from world religions.

As we read the Oxford stories collected from people all over the world and carefully archived at the Centre, we were able to connect to other religions well beyond our Judea-Christian sample. In reading these stories, we found thirty areas of congruence between their story themes and ours which pointed to an unexpected and remarkable unity of spiritual experience. We were dazzled by this discovery; awestruck by the eagerness of these diverse people to share their words and stories so freely; and staggered by the potential implications of this revealed unity.

Bobbie's simple question was transformed into an immense study of an interfaith, international group with remarkably similar experiences of the presence and action of God in their lives. It was an indescribable, unexpected journey, filled with three thousand amazing surprises, (read GOD) and utterly life changing for us!

Surely we had opened a door to the generosity of God who always gives us more than we can envision or imagine. We had stumbled upon an unexpected universal language of spiritual healing, not in intellectual, theological language, but in the stories of ordinary life experiences that people told us.

It was a treasure that had to be shared.

2

Surprises And Numbers

Lew and I were traveling down Interstate 95 between Philadelphia and Baltimore a few months into the project. Since we were always in a hurry, having to do the project in our spare time, this was no exception. We stopped at an oasis along the road to get gas, coffee, a Mrs. Field's cookie—and a map, expecting to accomplish this in a minimum amount of time. Mission almost completed, we stood before the "map man", and I made my request. "Could I please have a map of Baltimore?" He looked at me, paused and then answered, "What for?" A bit stunned by his response, I persisted. "Because we're going to Baltimore". That seemed like the proper response. This time, he responded with a bit more energy and volume, but with the same comment: "What for?"

The stress of the trip caught up with me and without thinking or monitoring my response, any pretense of politeness removed, I replied, "Because we're taking a spiritual healing project to four churches in Baltimore" ... with a silent 'so there' just beneath the surface. This time he responded with a clarity that astonished us and which would define our project in three short statements:

1. *Spiritual Healing happens all the time.*

2. *And it's happening right now while the three of us are talking.*

3. *And I feel better!*

And we had the presence of mind to pick up the pieces of our lives and remind him that we still needed a map of Baltimore. I think he gave us one!"

◆   ◆   ◆

We happen to like this story because it encapsulates all we were to learn throughout the project and it occurred at the very beginning of our journey. Beyond all that, it certainly was a surprise!

But of course the very first surprise was the response we got to our mailing, both in quantity (96%) and the implication that many people were actually interested in the subject of spiritual healing in the United Church of Christ. Later we would find the same responsiveness in Episcopal, Catholic and Reform Jewish Congregations. What this certainly hinted at was the presence of a "hidden" population within mainstream religious congregations who had a great deal to say about spiritual healing, in spite of what anyone thought.

We would soon discover that these people were not so much hidden as they were silent. Given the opportunity to share their words and stories about spiritual healing, their response was overwhelming and nearly unstoppable. Another surprise!

So what did they have to say?

When we asked people to share the words they associated with the words, "spiritual healing", the first thing we noticed was the commonality of words people were using. From Protestant to Catholic to Reform Jewish congregations, where we expected to see differences, we found the same words recurring. One word stood out as the most frequently used word to describe the experience of spiritual healing. That word was **"Peace"**, that deep sense of peace that "passes all understanding".

Interestingly enough, the word "peace" does not describe an emotion, but rather a state of being. In the themes and texts of their stories, we saw that most people were describing a change of state which was best summed up by the word, "peace".

When we asked for stories, we unexpectedly found a common definition of spiritual healing: **Spiritual Healing is an experience of the presence or action of God which is transforming.** And by transforming, people meant that God had become *real* to them. We were totally unprepared to find this common theme between such diverse groups of people, especially in the midst of powerful creedal differences. Another surprise!

While the stories were varied in subject matter, they fell within three classes: (1) Stories of the physical curing of disease, probably the most common association with the phrase, "spiritual healing", (the so called "miracle stories"): *"The cancer was there … diagnosed and all, but on the operating table, it was gone … completely disappeared".* (2) Stories of spiritual healing in which there was a disease present, but without a cure: *"In his dying, the whole family was somehow healed";* and (3) Stories of people who felt spiritually healed in the ordinary flux of life, sometimes with a stressor and sometimes without a stressor: *"I was late for church when I saw her standing by the door … she looked upset. Instead of going into church, I went over to her and said, 'are you ok?' Two hours later, we both felt healed …".*

The surprise here was that by far the largest number of stories were in the class of spiritual healing in every day life situations, in ordinary circumstances, with or without a stressor. When people became aware of the presence or action of God, their lives felt transformed.

It's also important to note here that the people who shared their stories felt quite clear about God's presence and action and the transforming nature of that experience. There was no ambiguity or uncertainty in their stories. *"Now I see my life in Technicolor—before it was only black and white!"*

The use of the word **transformation** is critical to understanding the experience our people described. They did not say that they were "changed" which would be a quantitative measure of the experience, meaning they felt more or less of something or some emotion. But the word "transformation" talks about a change of state which is a qualitative change meaning they entered into a "different place" than before the experience. God becoming real in one's life is that different place. This distinction will become essential when we look in greater depth at seeing life through the lens of spiritual experiences.

Our sample also saw their lives differently after their experience of the presence or action of God and used different words and different measurements to describe their lives. They were participating in a new reality which superseded the old reality and gave them different answers to the questions and issues that life was presenting them. *"I'd never seen my daughter in that light before. It transformed our relationship."*

Yet, they did not readily share their stories with others, including friends, spouses or family members. And for the most part, they had not shared them in their religious community. Reasons given for not sharing such stories usually centered around the fear that they would be seen as weird, crazy or too religious if they spoke about their experiences publicly. No surprise there! Talking about spiritual issues is like talking about money, politics or sex. It carries too much of a potential for judgment and criticism.

Later the hard data from our questionnaires would expand that observation. When specifically asked, people indicated they would be willing to share their stories in their religious congregations. But in fact they were rarely asked. We often heard, *"This is the first time anyone's ever asked me to tell my story."*

One final surprise! Clergy of all traditions were the group least comfortable talking about their own personal experiences of the presence or action of God in their lives. This was an unexpected taboo which had the unfortunate result of making the subject unspoken and unavailable for the congregation. If you don't hear it from the pastor, you're probably getting a subtle message that it's better not to talk about certain spiritual issues here. As one pastor shared with us, *"We're tough! Don't ask us to talk about that sort of thing in public. We just won't."*

OK, So where are we and what are we trying to help you see?

First, the element of **surprise** was an important part of people's experiences. They were "surprised" by the unexpected presence and action of God in their lives while they were in the process of going about their ordinary living. The experience was like a sudden shift of perception, awareness, or understanding. *"I looked for God in church and found God in my closet … that's where it happened."*

Even those people who were praying for some intervention from God were often surprised by what followed. *"A Christian woman of middle years had a son who developed leukemia. She was determined that he not only get the best possible medical treatment, but that she would cover all the spiritual bases as well. She started one prayer group in her church and then another and then two others in the same town and another two or three in various parts of the country, all praying that this young man would be cured of his disease. In spite of all this activity, he got worse and worse. As his condition deteriorated, she got more and more uptight and obsessed with his cure.*

One day, she decided that she was going to have it out with God and straighten God out. And so she prayed to God and found herself saying, 'God you don't know what it's like to be a mother and have a son who is dying!' And then she stopped and realized what she had just said. So she said, 'Well, I guess you do know what it's like to have a son who is dying … because you did … and he did … and you had the power to prevent that, if you wanted to … but you didn't'.

And then she stopped and said, 'All right, I give it up. If he lives, you know that's what I want more than anything. But if he dies, that's all right too'. And in that moment she was healed. All of the angst, all the insistence on outcome, all of the stress of having it her way was gone. And was replaced by a deep sense of peace." (Six months later her son remitted. But that is a different story.)

What is significant about this particular story is the surprise that *she* was the one who was healed, even though she was unaware she was in need of healing and clearly praying for some one else to be healed. She gave up the outcome of the situation and allowed God's solution to the problem, not hers. The concept of trying to control a situation by a variety of means and then letting go of the outcome were common threads in many of the stories we collected.

Second, the **experiences** people reported were all about the common recognition of the presence and/or action of God in their lives. In spite of the broad diversity of this sample (ethnic, socioeconomic, geographic, gender, preference, creedal), such agreement certainly talks about a universal and commonplace experience. No one tried to define "God" but used the word, "God" as the chief "actor" in their story.

Our sample told us God stories, almost always using the word, "God", but occasionally using the name "Jesus" or other words like "Lord" or "Creator". However the context of all the experiences was an encounter with the "deity" in the moment, no matter what name was given.

This leads us to suspect that you've already had such an experience in your life and know just what we're talking about. Or, you've had such an experience but have not recognized it as such, or you've decided to file it away under the heading of serendipity, chance, or luck.

For those of you who like to see specifics, here are some of our numbers from the people who filled out our questionnaires.

1. **Over 90%** reported having at least one experience of spiritual healing according to their definition of spiritual healing.

2. **97%** wanted to learn more about spiritual healing.

3. **96%** wanted more opportunities to talk about spiritual healing in their religious communities.

4. **83%** of our participants were between the ages of 35—75.

5. **74%** were female, and **26%** were male.

6. **47%** had been members of their particular religious community for over 15 years; **30%** had been members of their particular religious community between 5 and 15 years, making this a very stable sample in terms of organized religious life.

7. **All** respondents had support systems, friends and family reported as primary support systems, making the sample one of people connected to a variety of support systems rather than isolated individuals.

8. Over **three thousand people** have participated in the Spiritual Healing Project and its sequel, the Spiritual Aging Project, making this a remarkably large data collection. Our questionnaires have all been data processed at Johns Hopkins University School of Medicine, Center for Learning and Health and analyzed at the University of Pennsylvania.

Now the numbers from our participants that we really want you to consider are these:

1. **82%** reported a change in their "self identity, their understanding of who they are" as a result of their spiritual healing.

2. **91%** reported their experiences of spiritual healing had changed/transformed their lives.

3. **89%** reported having experiences of spiritual healing between the ages of **30 and 59.**

These first two findings relate to how your inner and outer life changes after an experience of the presence or action of God in your life. Changes in self identity and the way one lives one's life offer important information about your own developing spiritual life.

The third finding that nearly 90% of our participants have had an experience of spiritual healing between the ages of 30-59 redefines those years as critical years for spiritual development. We'll talk a lot more about that finding in Chapter VIII: The Critical Years.

Finally, we'd like to give you a summary picture of what we learned.

* As noted before, we started our data gathering by asking people to supply us with words, in a free association way, they would associate to the phrase, "spiritual healing."

These words were carefully and lovingly transcribed. The following list shows the most frequently used words in our study, arranged alphabetically.

Spiritual Healing is:

Acceptance

Belief

Comfort

Discipline

Energy

Faith

Grace

Hope

Integration

Joy

Knowledge

Love

Mystery

Newness

Openness

Peace

Quiet

Reconciliation

Surrender

Trust

Understanding

Victory

Wholeness

Yes!

That's the list: The basic vocabulary of spiritual life in our study. Within all the diversity of our sample, those words are fundamental to the stories we heard and the roots from which spiritual life grows. When you read them slowly, and even out loud, they become a kind of spiritual mantra.

* The words themselves probably represent some fragment of experience that people had in relation to those words. This was further shown by the fact that stories flowed immediately and easily after the words were shared. It was as if the words were a powerful springboard for the stories. If you had a word, then you probably had a story behind that word.

* The stories described experiences which occurred in the midst of life, with or without a stressor. The person having the experience of the presence or action of God did not cause the experience to happen. "It" happened to them, outside of their control.

* The experiences served as an introduction to a new state of being in which God's presence was experienced and God became real.

* Experiencing the presence and action of God in one's life implies there is a state of being which can be described as spiritual which defies rational explanations or causalities.

* This new state of being allows people to see life in an unexpected and profoundly different way.

* Within the experience/story, God was the "subject" of the story, even though the experience happened to the person involved. People were telling us "God" stories, not "me" stories.

* People indicated their self identity (their sense of who they were) was transformed by these experiences.

* They spoke eloquently of the multitude of life changes that had taken place after their experience of spiritual healing.

* They were moved to share their experiences but found it difficult to find a venue where that could take place (even in their families, marriages, with friends or in religious communities). Their reluctance was based on the fear they would be seen as weird, crazy or too religious.

* However, given the opportunity to share these experiences in a safe context (which we were able to provide), they were eager and more than willing to share them and the depth of feelings the stories contained. The stories were not forgotten, nor the power of the experience. In fact, in the telling of their stories, the original depth of the experience became a part of the present moment, often expressed with tears, not of sadness but of the power and meaning of the original experience.

* People looked for ways to express their gratitude for their experiences in a variety of loving actions toward others.

* People hearing the stories of others were often moved to discover their own stories of God present in their lives, which was a transforming moment for them as well.

* In the group setting, people reported feeling healed simply by being a part of the group

* In fact, the group itself seemed to be transformed in the experience of sharing words and stories about God. Signs of this transformation were that people stopped doodling, coughing or in general being somewhat distracted and instead began to pay close attention to what was being said. They didn't offer explanations or causalities, rather choosing to simply listen and not comment. People often said, "I've known you for 25 years and you've never told me that story". Or frequently people noted, "I've been a member of this community for over 30 years, and this is the first time I've ever told my story."

* One of the most important outcomes of our study was the finding that there were very few differences between our groups (Catholic, Protestant and Reform Jewish) in their reports of their experiences of the presence or action of God. This became particularly visible when we looked at the Alister Hardy archives of world religions extending beyond the Judea-Christian tradition and found similar data.

* What we thought might be a study of religious experiences in religious congregations turned out instead to be a collection of people's spiritual experiences, independent of religious preference, who just happened to be interviewed in a religious building.

* In looking at our data, one could not find any "ten steps" (or any number) which would *guarantee* a spiritual healing. It is clear the experience of healing was a product of God's initiative and presence and not anything the person had done to ensure such an outcome.

* The universality of this experience is staggering in its impli-cations and its potential for healing dialogues between people. If you take nothing else away from this book, this unity of spirit exists as a healing reality in a broken world. Religious differences are transcended by a universal spiritual reality available to all people

Our sample of ordinary people described the extraordinary presence of God in their lives with stories filled with power and clarity. If God can happen to them, we are convinced that God is present and available to all of us. The real question is whether we will open our *own eyes, ears and heart* and recognize the presence of God in our lives.

If you're not convinced yet about the ubiquitous presence of God, let's first talk about the nature of stories and then take a look at some of the stories of people who have recognized the presence and action of God in their lives and see what they have to tell us.

3

Stories: Our Way Of Life And Pathway To God

We are born story tellers. Many of our conversations with others are told in a story form. The reason for this is that we can't tell people our *experience*, we can only tell a *story* about our experience. Usually in a story, we are the "subject" of our story and by implication the story not only relates our experience, but something about us as a person and the way we deal with life.

In fact our normal questions to each other invite a story reply. To a spouse's question, "how did things go today?", we generally respond in a story form about what happened during the day. The elements of the story would be the events, how we felt about them, how we evaluated them, and how we behaved in relation to our feelings and our evaluation

Within our work settings, we generally tell a story to set the context and quality of our product or service. ("Here's how this product/service will make your business more profitable".) Within the family, stories are the medium of exchange as we share remembrances of the past; stories about the present; hopes and dreams for the future.

There is, however, a separate class of stories which are involved when one talks about spiritual matters. These are spiritual stories and as such they are stories about God. For example, in stories about the presence or action of God in one's life, the subject of the story is God, not you or me. Even though the story happens to us, it is clear that the main actor of the story is God and that these are "God stories". In our study, the outcome of God stories is always transformation and new life.

In stories in which we are the "subject", the theme of these stories is generally some kind of action between us and the world. These stories about me generally have an ending which provides some kind of closure to the situation. But the God stories are almost always about beginnings, not endings, and hence the openness of the future is led by the Spirit and undefined.

We heard a marvelous variety of stories: short, long, simple, complicated, stressful, peaceful, experienced alone or with others. We've mentioned the general classification of stories we heard which fell into three groups: the cure of disease stories; the healing without curing the disease stories; and the healing in ordinary life without a disease present, with or without a stressor, which was the largest group of stories we heard. All of the stories dealt in some way with the recognition of God's presence or action and a deep sense of healing and transformation.

Throughout history, people have always used stories to describe significant or not so significant events in their lives. Religious texts contain countless stories of people's interactions with God which have been collected and told because of their power to move and inform us about God. The trouble with these stories is they appear to be miraculous events which could only occur to certain very special people, and simply not something that happens to ordinary people in ordinary life events, and certainly not including me.

The stories we collected turned out to be just as "miraculous" in nature as any sacred text because they were all describing the same thing: the unexpected and transforming presence of God in this present time, happening to ordinary people, just like you and me.

The stories in religious texts are stories from the past that have survived the passage of time. The stories in our study were generally shared for the first time when given the opportunity. While they also had the power to move and inform us about God, the stories in our study carried an immediacy that deeply affected every group. One cannot remain unaffected when one's friend or neighbor, or even a stranger, is sharing a pivotal story that has transformed their lives. This is a very different experience from reading a text.

We saw this happening again and again whenever people shared their stories with the group. The original transforming event was somehow communicated to the group in the telling of their story in such a profound way that people often said: "I feel healed simply by hearing your story". And so did we!

It's time to let some of our stories speak for themselves. With over a thousand stories from which to choose, this is just a sample.

"Last March my son contracted a difficult illness ... emotional in nature ... it seemed to make him more and more withdrawn and finally, he was unable to leave the house. I was really unhappy. Everything we tried was no help. We tried various doctors, different therapies, and the whole thing only got worse. I didn't know what to do, but I was really frustrated for him and for all of us.

Last summer, I went on a retreat. I had to get away. The harder I worked on getting a handle on his problem, the worse it got. Well, anyway, I was at this retreat and there was this dog there that I liked to play "stick" with. He recognized me and we started to play. I would throw the stick and he would fetch it. But then, after a few times of throwing and bringing back, the dog wouldn't release the stick. He just wouldn't let go. I was pulling, he was tugging ... and I was getting more and more frustrated.

Finally, I almost screamed at the dog. 'Scamper, if you would just let go, you'd have a lot more fun.'

When I said that it was like being hit by a lightning bolt. I realized that I was the one who had to let go. I had to let go of trying to fix my son's situation. I wasn't able to "play" at anything when all I could think about what how to make my son better. I had to let go and see what would happen. It absolutely changed my life. My son still has his problems, but I'm no longer obsessed with making him better ..."

◆   ◆   ◆

"In 1991, seven of us went up into the boundary waters at the U.S. and Canadian borders to do some fishing. During a sudden and very violent storm, we made for the nearest island and were just able to make it. But that wasn't the end of it ... we were all, every one of us, struck by lightning. After it happened, I was on the ground ... and not able to move. I lay on my back and looked up into the sky ... it seemed to open up and I had the feeling I was looking into another world ... maybe heaven ... and I knew that God was there. I realized that God wasn't finished with me yet ... then there was this light all around me. I can't explain any of it.

But then I looked at one of the others who was lying next to me and saw that he was having seizures. I was able to get up and go to him. I held him and helped him to wake up. The experience makes me feel very humble. We all survived! Even though it was seven years ago, we still get together to talk about it ... we could never forget it. It was such a powerful bonding and healing experience."

◆   ◆   ◆

"My daughter and I have not had the easiest of relationships. Somehow, we always ended up in some kind of squabble or fight. Nothing ever seemed to work between us. You know how that happens sometimes.

Well, when she was in college over the summer she worked at a camp for disadvantaged children in the East. Before she left home, we had a fight over her determination to marry a man who was quite unsuitable for her, at least in my opinion. I stewed about this for a while, and then I called her and asked if I could come out to visit her. She said she had one day off, and if I could make it on that day to come ahead.

As I got on the plane to fly out, there were a number of professional football players also getting on the plane. I thought to myself, I hope one of them does not decide to sit next to me. I wanted to be left alone to think about what I wanted to say to my daughter and to figure out how to get her to change her mind about this guy. I was really determined to straighten her out and I needed some time to get prepared.

Well, none of the football players sat next to me. But instead a tall, native American man sat down, and I reluctantly fell into conversation with him. We talked about spiritual books, and finally he asked me where I was going. I told him I was going East to see my daughter. And then he asked me what my daughter was doing. With some slight irritation in my voice, because I really didn't want to be talking to him about her, I said something about the fact that she worked at a camp for disadvantaged children. I wished he would leave me alone.

But then he said something that really caught me off guard ... he said, 'your daughter is a healer'. I was astonished by his words. I had never thought of her this way before. His statement seemed to open up my whole being ... my entire orientation toward my daughter changed in that instant.

It was such an incredible experience that I wouldn't have been at all surprised if he simply dematerialized when we got to the airport, instead of walking off the plane. As for my daughter and me ... well we never got around to talking about her boyfriend.

Our whole relationship was changed ... and healed."

◆   ◆   ◆

"I just have to say that something is happening here in this group tonight that is very healing. I really appreciate being here tonight. I wasn't planning on coming ... but I did. I came in from about fifty miles away ... and this experience has turned out to be terribly important to me. There is healing happening right here ... I can feel it."

◆ ◆ ◆

"Most of my life I have spent in some diet regimen or another. I have gained and lost over a ton in that time. Last year, I started to gain again and it began to affect me physically as well as emotionally. My sister-in-law got me the Cleveland diet, but that didn't work. Finally, I went to an "expert" who told me what to do. I gained six pounds on his diet. I was beside myself, ... desperate and with no hope of ever changing the situation.

I stood on the scale, disgusted with myself, having eaten my way through the Super Bowl game and started to cry. I said to God, 'You'll have to help me, I can't do it.' And I meant precisely that.

Since then, I've lost thirty-four pounds and it's staying off. That moment on the scale was a transforming moment."

◆ ◆ ◆

"I think of this story as the 'event of the path'. I grew up Catholic, but had long ceased to practice it. My wife and I were at a resort in Oklahoma ... we were essentially non-religious at that time. We thought of ourselves as 'realists' and would make fun regularly of Oral Roberts and the faith healers on television.

I remember that the resort was named 'Shangri-La'. Well, on Sunday, as I was heading for the putting green, I passed a worship service going on in a room in the hall where I was walking. The door was open. I stopped, not intending to go in ... and then something just drew me into the room. I sat down, stayed through the service, and then went back to our room. I didn't go to the putting green. Instead, I saw my wife and told her that something had 'clicked'.

The next day, I found out that my grandmother had died at the exact moment that I went into that worship service. This impressed both of us ... and we made some jokes about connections, I guess to cover our feelings. But it turned out to be a healing experience for both of us.

We started to go to church regularly, and although we didn't talk a lot about it, our state is really different. We didn't feel we had to analyze it ... but just to go with it. And we have. And we really are changed!"

◆ ◆ ◆

"My first brush with death as an ordained minister was when I was invited by a family to be present to their dying mother ... a woman I had known before I was ordained. I was very nervous about visiting her ... what would I say? What did I know about death? How could I be helpful when I was so nervous?

When I arrived, she was peaceful and ready to die. She had waited for her family to all get there and I watched as I saw them relate to her ... I'm sorry, I can't tell this story without tears. I realized that while this was happening in the family, I was being healed too. The love simply flowed from her and flowed back to her from her family. It was God's love that was flowing between all of us. She was being loved as she died.

I still have a total sense of that day which was an unbelievable experience for me, and it transformed my ministry. The memory is as alive today as it was then. I will never forget it."

◆ ◆ ◆

"When my husband died in his early fifties, I thought I handled it OK ... what can you do? But after a while, I wasn't feeling well physically. I got scared so I went to the doctor who examined me and said, 'there's nothing wrong with you ... you are just grieving'. He said something that sounded like I should go home and grieve. But I didn't go home. I didn't feel good and I didn't want to be alone.

Instead, I stopped by a restaurant that we had visited a few times when my husband was alive. We went there for coffee ... sometimes a meal. The waitress came over to me. I had seen her before at the restaurant, but didn't know her. I recognized her, but I was not feeling especially friendly.

She said to me, 'You're not feeling well are you?' I nodded, surprised that she had noticed. And then she said the most incredible thing. She said, 'Would you like me to pray for you?' I was really taken aback, but thought for a moment and figured she meant she would include me in her prayers that night, or at church on Sunday or something like that. So I said, 'Yes'. She must have known what I was thinking because she said to me, 'No, I mean right here, now. I'd like to pray for you right now'.

I hesitated and then I nodded. I wasn't sure I could speak. She took my hands and there in the middle of that crowded restaurant, she prayed the most eloquent prayer I had ever heard. It was so beautiful, I felt a marvelous calm.

I was healed ... right there."

◆ ◆ ◆

"The judgment of others no longer affects me because of my relationship with God. It is really an authentic relationship. I was very grateful for my spiritual heritage being raised in a Midwest Quaker home. It was very important to me. But being a gay person, I felt spiritually abused by the church ... being a Christian seemed to be based on what you did not do ... what you shouldn't do.

After a lot of hard times and painful experiences, I came to realize that that wasn't true. I said to my mother, 'there is so much more to being a Christian than all the don'ts.' This made me feel a little more healed. Maybe it was the beginning of my healing ... Life seems to be allowing God to heal me ... sometimes physical, sometimes spiritual. But all the healings are so meaningful.

Ten years ago, a very dear friend was dying of AIDS. When I heard about it, I talked to the minister and he asked what the church could do for him. He had support from doctors, psychologists and support groups. But my friend said, 'I have no one to say my prayers with.' That was the beginning of the HIV support group here.

There have been many healings over the years ... not cures, but real healings. My friend was in a hospice unit so we took communion to him. When it came time to pass the peace, I took his hand and said, 'Peace to you,' and my friend was able to say to me, 'Peace to you' ... before he died.

Sorry, I can't help crying over the memory of that time because peace took on a whole new meaning for me then, as did communion. It was so important. I've never forgotten it."

◆ ◆ ◆

"I was twenty-two and a full-blown agnostic. Science was my God. I was a biological sciences major and only believed in what I could prove and deal with. I threw out my entire Catholic baggage when I was eighteen. I resolved to live a good life and not set a bad example, but for the rest of it ... that religious stuff ... no way!

When I was in school, the electron microscope had just been invented. During one of my classes, I watched a film of the spermatogenesis of a grasshopper and watched mitosis occur. I was knocked out! I said without even thinking about it, 'There must be a God. There's no design without a designer!'

I openly wept and left feeling content ... I was healed in that moment."

◆ ◆ ◆

"It was a terrible shock when I got the news from my doctor that I had breast cancer. He said it was not an aggressive one, and so I decided to wait until the holidays were over before I had it removed. When my family heard the news, they decided to stay and help out, and my daughter who lives in Florida started a prayer chain in her church.

Finally, I went to the hospital. I was constantly checking my breast to feel the lump which was quite a large one and I was having a burning sensation in my breast. I was not happy with that new symptom, but put it down to stress. During that time, I also met with my pastor and he was very calming. I was able to pray, 'Whatever you want for me, God, that's what it will be.' When I prayed that prayer, I was engulfed by an overwhelming peace! It was very powerful.

An intern came into the room to check my breast the night before surgery and said, 'Where's your lump? I can't find it.' He decided that he was just tired and left. I didn't think too much about it. I was still feeling peaceful in spite of what was going to happen.

The next day, they prepared me for surgery. The surgeon came into the operating room and examined me. When he finished, he said, 'I can't feel the tumor. You'll have to go down to X-ray and get it imaged so I can get on with this.' When I came back from X-ray, the doctor said, 'I can't believe this. I'll do a biopsy, but I think we'll only remove some tissue. The lump is not there.'

I was anesthetized and the biopsy turned out to be benign. That was fifteen years ago. The doctors would not discuss the case with me. But I knew I had been healed by prayer ... by the prayer that I was able to pray ... and the prayers of others. The doctors wouldn't even listen to that ... but I knew."

◆　◆　◆

"Seven years ago, I was in the locked ward of a mental hospital. My husband had divorced me and my kids were gone ... both kids were addicts on the street somewhere. I was catatonic ... just lying on my bed ... it felt like returning to the womb. Everyone was giving up on me, but I didn't care. It felt wonderful ... comfortable ... safe ... warm ... nothing to do, nothing to worry about ... just being taken care of.

One day, I heard one of the doctors say that if they didn't get through to me in three days, they would lose me. I didn't care. What did I have to live for anyway?

That night, I was resting ... partly sleeping I guess ... when the door opened and I saw a figure standing in the light of the hallway. At first, I didn't know who it was ... it didn't look like any of the doctors or *people who worked in the hospital. Then I realized that it was Jesus standing there in the doorway. He looked at me and said, 'Get up! You can't go yet. Your children need you.'*

There was nothing meek or mild about that voice. It was tough, not nice at all. But I heard him, and I knew what I had to do.

The problem was that I was in a locked ward in a mental hospital. If I told the doctors that Jesus had come to me and told me to get up ... well I'm not sure I would ever have gotten out of the hospital

But I did get out ... I was able to convince them that I was all right. I was discharged. I went out and found my children and moved us all here. The kids are all right now ... off drugs and straight. We're a family again.

This is the first time I have ever told this story. I was too afraid people would judge me or think I was really crazy ... they wouldn't understand what happened to me. But I can tell it here because my love for God is so strong now, I am so strong now that I want to share what happened to me."

◆　◆　◆

"My son had broken his neck. I was in shock ... crushed ... desperately afraid. About 3:00 a.m. I said to God, 'I can't let go of him ... but if that's what you want, then you'll have to give me the strength to do it.'

I felt a great peace and was able to give up my control of the situation ... and my son was not only healed, he recovered fully."

◆　◆　◆

"I was diagnosed with a three-centimeter tumor in my right breast. I asked Jesus to heal me. When they did the surgery, they found that the tumor was gone. Not only that, there were clean margins all around the site.

I fell in love with God!"

◆ ◆ ◆

"When I was in Harvard Business School, I learned one of my profes-sors was dying of cancer. I hesitated ... not knowing if I should talk to him about it or not. But I decided to bring the subject up to him. He talked to me about his problem and thanked me for asking because he had found that he could not always talk to people about it. They simply didn't want to listen.

Listening can be healing ... it can heal into life or into death. Either way.

I realized that God is God and I am not ... and that has helped me to be healed myself."

◆ ◆ ◆

"My healing was in the form of an understanding between me and a young man of my age who was dying of leukemia. In the course of becoming his doctor, I also became his friend. We did not specifically talk about Jewish things. But the last time I saw him before he died, he took my hand and said, 'Thanks for taking care of me.'

I helped him, but he uplifted me. It was a healing without a cure."

◆ ◆ ◆

This is a small sample of the stories we heard and if you're not affected by them you'd better check your pulse to see if you're still alive! We have read and told these stories dozens of times. Each time we do, we remember the people who told them and the effect they had on the group as if it were happening at that time. That's the wonder of this kind of story. It reaches us on a different level and embeds itself in our heart and spirit.

The stories you just read tend to be intense and somewhat overwhelming in their nature. So, it might be a good time for you to take a break, and let your heart absorb what we've been telling you. You might also consider browsing through your own life and thinking about your own words and stories about the presence or action of God in *your* life.

If you'd like to do that, get comfortable, relax and let the phrase "spiritual healing" bubble through your consciousness. Just let any words come into your mind as they will. Call it word association or whatever works for you. Just remove the rules of proper or acceptable language and decide that each word or phrase is the right one. It is our experience that whatever words appear in your mind point to an openness to the presence or action of God of which you may or may not be aware.

Have pencil and paper ready. A small notebook would do nicely. Write whatever words come from your heart into your mind, unmonitored and uncensored. After you complete your first word list, let it be open to whatever other words occur to you over a period of time, the duration of which will make itself known.

When it feels like your list is complete, take a little time to muse on it—read it out loud if you like—share it with a friend if you want (always a good idea). Read it for several days just as a part of your daily life—and see if a story attaches itself to any of your words.

For many of you, a story or even several stories will be quite available. For some of you, a story which you may have forgotten or not associated with God's presence or action may appear. For those of you who say, "well I don't have a story", keep your word and story list handy to stimulate the process and then re-read the stories we've put in this chapter. If one speaks to you, borrow it as a gift from God and pay attention to what happens.

Write whatever story(ies) you have in as much detail as you can and start to keep a log of other stories that occur to you in the next few days or weeks. (There's no time requirements or limits for words and stories.) But remember, these are descriptions of **pivotal moments** when God became **real** to you—God Stories—not your life history or spiritual autobiography. (You can do those in another context.)

In the next chapter we'll talk about the various "Spiritual Themes" that appear in our stories. Maybe they will touch your own spiritual life.

4

Spiritual Themes

We've already talked about the remarkable unity in our stories, which was an ongoing and unexpected surprise to us. Further, with no instructions given as to what people *should* tell us, or how the stories *ought* to be structured, a number of themes spontaneously presented themselves within the overarching symbol of God Present or Active in ordinary life circumstances: surprise; surrender; acceptance; transformation; the experience of peace; a sense of gratitude; the experience of God's healing Presence and Love; the use of prayer in the healing process and the lack of emphasis on the role of suffering in situations of physical or emotional pain. Indeed, we often heard expressions of gratitude for one's illness as a part of the transforming process.

The themes could be interwoven, creating a powerful portrait of the experience of spiritual healing and transformed lives. They may resonate with your own experience(s) or serve as additional benchmarks in the process of discovering your own stories.

The theme of **surprise** was the anchor of the project. We were surprised at every turn by the growing presence and action of God that kept manifesting itself in the project and in the lives of those who shared their stories.

"This is a hard story to tell, and I've never shared it with anyone. For a long time, I just didn't know whether to believe it happened or not ... it was so strange. And yet, I knew that it did happen.

Six years ago I had lost touch with God and every thing was a mess. I was raised Catholic but I had fallen away and as things got worse and worse, I got more and more desperate. Finally, I asked God to help me

... I asked God every day to help me ... and nothing changed. I was furious. I felt that everything I had been told was untrue and that God didn't care.

Then one day for some reason, I don't quite understand, I began to think of all the things I had and I decided to go for a walk. As I was walking, someone grabbed my left hand. It felt good. I looked down, but there was no one there. But I knew that God had heard me and had reached out and held my hand to let me know that it would be OK ... and it was."

The nature of Spirit is such that when it breaks into the material world, it almost always seems surprising and unusual to us. Of course the Spirit is present all the time but it is the "break-ins" that attract our attention. The critical action is to recognize Spirit when it arrives at our doorstep and enters our heart. But we also need to name this event in some way so that we can retain it in our mind. The value of story is that it allows us to remember and also to communicate information about the event. *"But I knew that God had heard me ... and it was OK."*

Another recurrent theme was **surrender** or letting go of the outcome. From a strictly logical point of view, it is clear that if we insist that God should do what *we* know is best then there is no reason for God to be involved, except as a "servant" of our will. The inflexible insistence on *our* outcome was always an impediment to healing in our stories.

"I was trying to manage my son's drug addiction. I was furious with God for letting him get on drugs. One day I called home from where I worked and talked to his father who said, 'this is not the first time he's been on drugs'. He started to give me a hard time and I started to give him one back. We were both angry and frustrated with the situation which was out of control and that we couldn't change.

Then I heard God say, 'Sit down and shut up!' I did and then God said, 'Max needs his father' and I heard that too. Later, I went on a retreat and in the middle of it was able to let go and realize that God was taking me to a place where God wanted me to go, the place I needed to be. I needed to let go, and that was my healing."

The theme of **acceptance** is closely allied with the theme of letting go or surrender. But acceptance takes us to a new place beyond surrender. Surrender is an action, but acceptance is a state of being, one that may proceed from the action of surrender and becomes a part of one's life.

"I have two sons and they are both in jail. As if that wasn't bad enough, I got so involved in trying to get the right lawyers to get them out of jail I was running around like a crazy person. It was so expensive! I had to work all the time to get enough money to pay the lawyers. This went on for three or four years.

Then one day when I was visiting my youngest son, he said to me, 'You're in the wrong struggle, Mom. You're a Christian … you don't need lawyers. Pray to God. You're trying to control all of this. Give it up! I know I'm here for a purpose and I can trust God. I need to do my time … what I did was wrong.'

Suddenly, I knew he was right. Now I can let them go … and I can open up to others … I can tell them my story. My sons will be free when the time is right. It's all changed for me. I can let it go and trust God. It really is a healing … for me."

The theme of **transformation** was clearly perceived by our sample and is a cornerstone of all the experiences of the presence or action of God reported to us. Transformation is a change of state in which God becomes *real*, which is the entrance into a new paradigm of the meaning of one's life. That new paradigm sees our lives from the lens of the spirit which makes everything "new". ("I once was lost, but now I'm found".)

"Healing can be disconcerting and downright scary. I was a chaplain in a general hospital. A man in his 60's was admitted with an aneurysm. He was losing function and the family was called in. I was not involved with this part of it, but a day and a half later … after the family had assembled, I was asked to come in. He was in really bad shape and was having great difficulty breathing.

*The family asked me to pray for him. I said, 'OK tell me about him'.
They talked about him and then we held hands and prayed. I affirmed
his love of life and thanked God for the past few hours when the family
had gathered. I asked God for serenity for the family and asked God to
hold him in the palm of his hand. Then he stopped breathing. I thought
to myself, 'My God, I've killed him'. But then I realized it was just that
he had been healed enough to let go ... indeed. That he had just experienced the ultimate healing ... death.*

*I knew that God was active in this process. I saw death in a new
light. I finally learned to say, 'OK God, whatever you're going to do is
OK. I'll try to be there to go along with it.'*

It was a transformation for me ... I was healed too."

Peace is certainly the word used most often to describe the
state of being accompanying spiritual healing. Again, peace is
not an emotion, but a place or state one enters into. It is often
accompanied by a feeling of gratitude to God, the one who has
done the healing.

*"I thought you might appreciate this story. One year ago, I was in
the hospital waiting for a liver transplant. It felt like a very strange
time. Here I was, waiting for someone else to die so that I could have a
part of their body in order to live myself.*

*All I could do was to wait and hope ... and pray that I would live
long enough to receive the transplant.*

*But each day, I felt a little worse and a lot more anxious and fright-
ened. My wife and I had recently joined a church but we didn't really
know anyone there. So we felt very alone in this waiting period. But one
day, a get well card arrived from the church. I was really surprised. It
was the kind of card that says, 'we're thinking about you and praying
for you' and ... as I held the card, I felt an immediate sense of peace ...
and gratitude. I can't explain it. I was just holding the card, and I began
to feel different. The waiting became bearable. It was a real turning
point for me ... this sense of peace when nothing else had changed.*

Shortly after I received the card, I also received my new liver. I haven't rejected it yet ... And I may. But I will always remember that sense of peace. It was remarkable."

God's healing presence and love was the centerpiece of every story. As we have said before, the universal definition of spiritual healing was "the presence or action of God in one's life which was transforming." The clarity of understanding that this was "God present in my life" was the sub-text of every story.

"I know that touch may be healing. In 1990, my mother came to live with us. It soon became apparent that she had Alzheimer's Disease. We put her in a day care program but she simply got worse and worse. I went to a support group and it helped me in some ways. But pretty soon, my mother became house bound. She couldn't go to the day care any more and I could feel the pressure really building in me. I felt I was carrying everyone on my back and it was breaking under the strain.

I had to dress and undress her. She was incontinent so I had to clean her up. It was really tough. I spent a lot of time grieving over this ... the support groups were some help. I learned some coping techniques and tricks to make things work better. But then it got really bad. I felt absolutely alone. It didn't matter, though ... I still had to cope with the whole thing myself.

One day I was trying to get her dressed. I wanted her to brush her teeth so we could go to the doctor's office. She was impossible ... waving the tooth brush around, smearing tooth paste on the mirror. I knew I was losing it ... I couldn't help myself and I heard myself shouting at her ... 'you'll be the death of me'. I wanted to take that tooth brush and just jab it into her ... stab her with it. My mother was oblivious to me and my feelings. I was ready to snap.

Then suddenly I felt two huge hands upon my back. I was sure it was God. No one was in the room, but suddenly I was not alone. No words were spoken, but everything changed.

The anger drained away and I felt ... peaceful. Mother was just the same, but I was different.

Suddenly I could cope. I hadn't asked for help, but the help came just when I needed it.

To this day, that event makes everything possible in my life. Now I know I can talk with God, especially when things get hard. It was a healing for me, even though I know that my mother will only get worse."

Prayer is the common currency of spiritual activity and most prayers are petitionary in nature. We pray for what we perceive we need; we pray for others. We also pray in times of crisis, joy or gratitude or when we sense or hope there is something beyond our own self and our material world. It is probably the most common religious/spiritual action that people take and it takes as many forms as there are people.

"My son had been shot and I followed the ambulance to the emergency ward. When I got there, they told me he was dead. I said, 'I don't think so'. I walked into a corner of the hospital and I said to God, 'All my life I have believed in you, now prove it to me'. I went back to the room where my son was and the doctor said he was sorry but that my son was dead. And I said, 'I don't think so'. I went over to the table and I said to him, 'OK, the doctor says you are dead ... but I don't think so, so move your right arm.'

My son started to shake all over and I said, 'open your eyes'. He couldn't do that, although you could see his eyes rolling under his lids. The doctor said that was natural with dead people. But I said, 'I don't think so', and took his hand. I said, 'squeeze my hand and he did'.

The doctor couldn't believe it. My son not only survived, he now has two jobs. When you say there's nothing more I can do ... then God can make it happen. He was paralyzed, but now he can work two jobs. I know God healed him."

There was a surprising **lack of emphasis on suffering** in the stories that were told even though many people were obviously suffering either with the pain of a physical illness or in a state of emotional trauma or grief. Rather, the stories were about the presence and action of God and the transformation of the situation, even when the end of the story may have been the death of the individual.

The setting for this story was in a room which was filled with beautiful photographs all taken by the teller of the story ... who also happened to be blind.

"In 1991, I was told that I had a terminal illness and was given six to twenty-four months to live. I was a successful top corporate executive ... type A personality for sure. I cared nothing for anything other than myself ... My pleasure and my power. I was only for me ... self absorbed totally.

In the face of this disease, my life has miraculously turned around. I recognized the truth of the Gospel and was transformed. I was so ego-centric and self centered. But since I have become blind ... it's strange ... somehow all the women I meet are beautiful and all the men are good looking ...

I can only tell you how grateful I am for my disease because it has transformed my life. Even though the Gospels have been there all along, they were new to me. I am a different person.

And finally today, I can share with you what I've been afraid to share. I am dying of AIDS ... and I know you will not judge me. I couldn't share it before our meeting today."

Physical or emotional pain would often be the precursor of a new depth of spiritual awareness and understanding. Not that the pain caused this to happen, but rather it acted as an intense focus which superseded other less compelling issues. It was not uncommon to hear that people grew spiritually in those times when their lives were intensely involved in a highly charged, and painful situation.

In fact, pain pulls us back into ourselves, with an insistence that we pay attention to it. It's hard to ignore the incessant message that pain conveys. It distracts our attention from the world around us and profoundly focuses us on inner processes that are also at work.

"For two years I had intense back pain, so severe that I finally could barely walk.

Everything in my life was compromised by my pain. I went to doctor after doctor—tried alternate forms of medicine: chiropractic, acupuncture, Reiki, therapeutic massage … you name it—I tried it. Nothing worked. It was finally suggested that I face the fact I would end up in a wheel chair … No medical solution could possibly help my situation.

But at the same time that I felt about as low as you can get physically and emotionally … I was aware that my spirit was somehow growing … I can't explain it. Suddenly I found myself in a deeper spiritual place … it felt like each day I became more spiritually aware of God's presence in my life and in the world around me. It was as if right in the middle of the pain was the presence of God … and I knew that in a brand new way. It didn't change my pain … but somehow co-existed with the pain. And I was filled with gratitude."

Now to be grateful for one's disease or one's pain talks about a new way of looking at life from a spiritual standpoint. Ordinarily that kind of behavior would be viewed as crazy (literally) or simply inappropriate. But from a spiritual perspective, it reflects the true nature of the relationship between God and people. God's presence is always transforming, making everything new. Even disease and pain can enter a new and different place.

Many stories combined several themes in a powerfully orchestrated rendition of spiritual healing.

"Twenty seven years ago, I was awakened by a voice saying, 'After the operation, you will be all right'. Seeing as I was not sick, with no operation scheduled, I just forgot all about it. Some years later, I was diagnosed with pancreatic cancer. I was told that the surgery was very risky, the chances for survival almost zero. I had forgotten all about the voice so I just desperately tried to control my recovery. But I'd lost 40 pounds and was going downhill fast.

I prayed with a prayer group. The next day, they served communion and somehow, I don't know how, I just let go and said, 'OK' to the surgery. From the moment I surrendered, my life has been a blessing. I sur-

vived the operation. I was OK. I slowly got better. Now every morning, I wake up and say, 'thanks'. My life really started after the operation. The voice was right."

While this is one of the few prophetic stories we collected, it nevertheless embodies themes that are common to many stories of physical cure: the joining of a prayer group and praying for recovery with the group; the giving up of trying to control the disease; the moment of surrender, saying "yes" to everything, regardless of the outcome; as well as the common reaction that healing was the benchmark of a transformed life and a new beginning to which gratitude became a necessary response.

Finally, it is important to remember that some of our stories describe the experience of having a disease without experiencing a cure, but in which a spiritual healing was a powerful and unexpected outcome. We have certainly learned from our participants that the healing of the spirit transcends the curing of a disease.

In other words, if your measurement for healing is "cure", then you will automatically miss those gifts of healing which are spiritual in nature, though not representative of physical curing.

"My father was a minister and he spent a great deal of energy working for the church. Then he had a heart attack which left him blind and disabled. He was given six months to live, but he lived 16 years. From this affliction, he made an amazing transition to becoming accepting of his limitations. He assumed a different form of ministry, becoming a spiritual adviser and counselor and saw this new ministry as the "gift" of his affliction.

I was deeply affected by the change in him and decided to go into the ministry myself. We were both healed ... each in our own way."

This story talks about the idea of illness as a "gift" rather than a problem and affirms the experience of the healing of others in contact with a patient who is spiritually healed, though not physically cured. Other stories tell of whole families feeling "healed" as a result of an experience in which curing did not take place.

Collectively, all the themes we've talked about (surprise, surrender, acceptance, transformation, peace, gratitude, God's healing Presence and Love, prayer, seeing illness or pain as a gift) pointed people toward a new way of looking at their experiences which was almost always followed by unexpected outcomes which turned out to be life changing in nature. Being open to the possibility of God present in any situation opens the door to a new spiritual self-awareness and identity.

When God becomes *real*, anything can happen!

5

Unexpected Outcomes And Transformed Lives

Some of the most important findings from our data came from two questions which examined the transformation that took place in people's lives, after these pivotal experiences of God's presence. The first question dealt with issues of self awareness and identity. **"Has your understanding of who you are (your self identity) changed since your experience of spiritual healing? If yes, please describe the change(s)."** As we mentioned earlier, 82% of those who filled out our questionnaire indicated "yes", indeed their self image had changed. We'd like some of their responses to speak for themselves in their own language of healing. We have arranged them according to their religious preference:

Episcopal:

I believe more sharply that God loves me and that I am created in God's image.

I am more compassionate, less judgmental, calmer, more centered, more aware of my precious fragility.

I am stronger and know I can get through most things with God's help and my own.

The giving over of all of who I am to God, both light and shadow, providing more acceptance of God's love and the peace that passes all understanding.

I know that I am loved unconditionally which empowers me to be what God intends for me to be.

My priorities are entirely different. God is my top priority now.

I am a servant of Christ—before I was a martyr.

I am more patient, more aware of my weakness, but paradoxically I am stronger somehow.

I feel I am more a part of God and God's creation, rather than being alone.

I have come to accept myself for whom God wired me up to be—not for who I or anyone else thinks I should be.

Catholic:

I know that I am a child of God, loved by God, one of God's beloved.

I feel accepted and forgiven by God.

I feel more loving and patient.

I am definitely more relaxed and more open to others and to life.

This has made me more relaxed and gentle, definitely less fearful.

I now feel more spiritually mature.

I am empowered and transformed.

I am filled with purpose.

I am less angry, and more giving to others.

I feel I can live and be rooted in the present. I value the present moments in my life more than I ever did before.

I recognize each moment as an opportunity to see God acting in the NOW.

United Church of Christ:

It is a constant process. I am more loving, confident, accepting.

I am more relaxed and less fearful of the future.

I am more at peace with myself

Steady growth in sensitivity and understanding of my purpose in life.

I realize more strongly that I am one of God's children.

I am imperfect, but still loved.

I can forgive myself for some of the unspiritual things in my past.

I recognize and accept that God can use me.

I can honor the dark nights of my soul, embracing them so as to go through them.

I am more comfortable with letting people see who I am. I do not feel as though I have to put up a front.

Reform Jewish:

I learned to appreciate the "now" of my life; to value the present, not was or will be.

I am more aware of myself as a spiritual being.

I feel more peaceful and self sufficient.

I now know what's important and can look beyond certain situations at the "big picture of things".

I've added a more complete dimension to who I am.

I am able to see myself as part of the whole, and committed to others and to God.

I am more sensitive to others; I encourage more spiritual encounters.

I now allow myself to do this ... "experience my spiritual self"—whereas before I was not in tune with it.

It has made me grateful for many blessings and made me strive to help others.

It has helped me to share my peace.

I am more calm and confident; more at peace with myself.

I have become a better listener in my own life and to others.

I am more humbled to the world.

I am more understanding of others and less angry.

Clearly, people reported a strong sense of God's presence and participation in their lives after their spiritual healing. Their orientation to life became more rooted in the present; more filled with peace and confidence; less contentious; less ego-bound and more directed toward others. Their sense of self is less demanding as people understood themselves to be rooted within God's presence and action, rather than their own. Hence they are freer to move through life in less constricted ways, more open to the uncertainties of life without being overcome by them.

It is interesting to note that reductions in states of anger and stress, the increasing sense of peace and comfort as well as a reaching out toward others were all described as accompanying features in these changes in self identity. One could not help but be aware that all of these descriptions would be considered as healthy and desirable qualities and also might serve as a description of a new state of being called: spiritual health.

The second question deals with changes in one's life after an experience of spiritual healing. **"Generally speaking, has your spiritual healing changed your life? If yes, please describe the change (s)."** As we noted earlier, 92% of those who filled out the questionnaire indicated that their life had most certainly changed. Here are some of their responses.

Episcopal:

God is a major influence in everything I do.

More meaning, more beauty, more awareness of God's compassion and elegant Grace.

A greater awareness of the times when I am really centered and a greater desire to seek that out.

It has given me proof that selfish thinking is harmful, not only to myself but also to others.

It was a mountain top experience in my closet (that's where it happened!) I have utter confidence that God is with me in times of stress and distress.

I am changed not radically, but it has been integral to my continuing transformation.

My past career was as a financial services consultant. My future career will be focused around the church.

A healed marriage; a healed psyche; a life filled with possibilities rather than failures.

As I continue to be present to God and allow God to do what God will with me, I am becoming more healthy.

I grew in understanding from "I" to "we".

I expect my spiritual healing to continue to change my life and to help me to be open to God's direction.

It has made me look for God in many places.

A new path; greater faith; a growing understanding.

I am quicker to obey those spiritual promptings or leadings.

I am more confident and honest with myself. I am willing to fail.

I am more willing to let God be the driver and me the passenger.

It's the difference between believing and knowing. I feel that I know God and Jesus rather than just assenting to a belief.

I'm open to Grace and not just the Law.

Without it, I would be a whole different person.

Catholic:

I felt less controlling about my life. I've given over the control of my life to God.

I am more open to my neighbor(s) and more anxious to serve them in some way.

Life is a richer, fuller experience for me now.

Spiritual healing has given me life in "Technicolor!"

I am spending more time in my devotional life, in prayer and worship.

I have gone back to the church.

I feel I am living my life for God. I want to be the person God wants me to be.

Knowing God's will for my life is now more important than ever.

I can let go of the past and live in the present.

I believe that God acts right here in the present moment. I want to be a part of that action by providing loving service to others.

I am now able to love beyond myself.

Putting it at a basic level, the essence of life as simple: To pray more; to thank God more and to try to help others.

United Church of Christ:

Most importantly, I find it has influenced the decisions I have made.

I am much more patient and tolerant of others' differences.

I am willing to allow others to have opinions without trying to change them.

I feel more love and compassion and empathy toward others.

I can concentrate more on improving my own life rather than telling others how they should change to suit me.

I just know I must have a stronger faith.

These changes give me more faith, openness to more of God—Growth!

I am no longer a victim.

I have more humility. I am much more willing to rely on God.

I have been freed from captivity which has increased my gratitude for all things and my awe of the mystery of God.

I am not afraid about the future.

I am less fearful, more energetic, able to concentrate more, less afraid of trying to be honest, more empathic, more open, seeking growth experiences, a better listener.

I have more courage to go into and through another round of pain.

I've tried to be a better person, to go out of my way to help a friend.

I like and respect myself … I show an interest in people and in helping and I consider myself a giver and not a taker.

I am more comfortable with spirituality.

My sense of "call" has been confirmed and that makes it easier to face some of the tough experiences in life and to make hard choices.

It has given me inner peace.

Everything has changed: my attitudes, my relationships, and most of all my awareness of God's presence in all of life.

Reform Jewish:

I now give more to others.

I am more aware of time and can control my feelings faster.

I am a happier person.

I feel quite fortunate to have the comfort and strength that has been given to me during prayer times and the times when I've experienced spiritual healing.

I have embraced my experiences of spiritual healing and take comfort from them without question.

It has enriched my life. I can accept the losses in my life and appreciate each day and count my blessings.

I feel more comfortable with who I am and in relationship with others.

I have more faith in God. I pray much more often and thank God more often for everything.

Everything I experience on a spiritual level changes me.

I have a sense of wholeness and a better sense of how I fit into the universe.

It has brought peace into my life.

I am more comfortable dealing with crises and better able to express my feelings.

It has changed my outlook, my reactions and how I deal with situations.

I am more in tune with myself and others; more giving; and more open to receiving.

I am spending more time being still and less busy. And I spend more time with my family.

I am easier to live with and less judgmental of others.

I am more compassionate and I recognize the gift in all things.

I am calmer, quieter and more peaceful.

I am far more content; happier and grateful one thousand times a day for the smallest of blessings and for the thousand moments of joy.

Several powerful themes are repeatedly visible. People felt a greater reliance upon what they perceived God wanted for them in a given situation. People also reported being less self involved and ego bound and more open to others. They felt a deeper sense of calm, peace and confidence about their lives and the future. They had achieved a kind of simplicity about life that was less complicated and more spiritually centered.

They reported feeling more compassionate and less judgmental and critical of others. They were more comfortable with themselves as spiritual people, felt happier and more content. They felt directed to be helpful toward others in many different ways and situations. They appeared to be more accepting of the reality of limitations and to see themselves and others in a more realistic light.

You will notice that people did not report that their external circumstances were somehow improved or that life suddenly became joyous or uncomplicated. The transformation they experienced was spiritual and not material. In other words in their every day life they did not suddenly find magical solutions to their problems. They did, however, find a spiritual dimension to their lives which had a profound impact on their external, material life.

These were people who were more than willing to take actions in the world that were helpful and compassionate in nature. Helping others through acts of service is a persistent theme in the reported changes in their lives.

Because they were less afraid about the future, the reality of change did not appear to be threatening. They were more focused on living in the present moment, being open to God, and living within a spiritual center, rather than a material one. They appeared to be more confident about their spiritual lives: It's the difference between believing and knowing.

When one sees the world through the lens of Spirit, life is transformed, not as we might have chosen or sought, but surely altered and healed by the experience of God present and active in all of life.

Take another look at these wonderful statements when you have the time. We think you'll be struck by the marvelous integrity and similarity of the statements between religious traditions. As we said of the word list we shared with you earlier, you simply do not find religious differences in these experiences. They appear to come from one source and one people sharing marvelous moments with God.

So where have we been and where are we now?

We've had a chance to share with you the experiences of some three thousand people, most of whom report that they have had an experience in which God became real to them. Further, we've given you a mix of words, data and stories that details the experience and shows the effect of these experiences on people's lives.

We have also noted the remarkable similarity of experiences. The words, stories, data and the overarching themes all speak of a common ground that transcends ethnic, socioeconomic, geographic and even creedal boundaries. It was generally impossible to identify in which faith community these experiences occurred.

We could have thrown the stories on a table and you could not have selected the Protestant from the Catholic or from the Jewish ones, unless there was a specific religious reference, e.g. Father, Rabbi, etc. But these references tended to be circumstantial to the stories rather than reflecting a religious orientation.

What we thought was to be a religious study of different faith communities, vis à vis the experience of spiritual healing, turned out to be the stories of people who had been spiritually transformed, told to us within a building used for religious purposes. This was reinforced in a much more comprehensive way when we looked at the Alister Hardy Religious Experience Research Centre data and found such similarity of themes between our stories and the stories from all the other world religions archived in that location.

We cannot help but be convinced that this experience is truly universal.

So what does that mean to you, the reader? It means that you can not opt out of the possibility of this experience in your life simply on the basis of some technicality that you belong to a sub group to which it doesn't apply. Our data are simply too overwhelming for that excuse.

Or you may be saying, "I've never had such an experience … so I don't know what you're talking about". Or, you might very well be saying: "OK, that's fine. I get it. All I need to do is to have an experience with the presence or action of God in my life and I'll be transformed. So … give me the program, and I'll be happy to follow it. Give me the ten steps or whatever it takes and that will be the end of it … right?"

And we would say, "No, it's not that simple". We have presented these data and stories to show you that God is present and active in the world all the time. This ubiquitous God offers us the chance to look at our life in an entirely different way and see it from a spiritual standpoint, and not simply a psycho/social/historical world view (a material standpoint).

Our goal is to help you see this as an outgrowth of our data and experience. Our mission is to help you open your "spiritual eyes" and see *your own life as the arena of transformation* and to discover *your own stories* of those moments when God became real to you.

The stories we were told point out what happens when the Spirit breaks into our material life. They represent beginnings, not endings, operating as an open door to the marvelous creation of Spirit entering our lives. Hearing these powerful stories is the easy part. We can connect to the participants, feel the drama of change and transformation and recognize our lives in some of the stories.

However, our participants also stood at the edge of a new way of looking at their lives in general and their spiritual lives in particular. For them the experience was transposed into a new and transformed life, most likely unsought, but which would change the course of their history. These were turning points in a life dictated by material needs and services and transformed into a spiritual life in which God is present in every moment and in which every experience can be transformed by seeing it with spiritual eyes rather than material eyes.

Yet, the question is not simply, "will you see God in your life?" There is a difference between seeing God in our lives and evaluating those experiences in *our* terms. This is particularly important for those experiences that are painful or tragic and which call up our feelings of what ought to happen in a given situation or what is "right" according to our wishes or understanding. When we ask, "Why did God allow this to happen?", we are assuming that we know better than God and shifting the focus of the experience from God to us. Clearly this activity is not the same as being open to the Mystery of God present and active in the world.

The real question is whether we will give up trying to define what God *ought* to do and allow ourselves to experience what God actually **is.** Can we allow God to ultimately transform every corner of our existence until our very life is an expression of God in the world?

Perhaps at its most basic level, the central question is whether we will say "Yes" to God, and discover an unfamiliar spiritual life in the midst of our familiar and comfortable way of living, which calls us occasionally to be religious. We'd say that given the statements people supplied to us, it is a life beyond anything they could have thought about or planned and even more. The God our people encountered was a God of generosity and abundance and surprise.

Our data have provided a powerful look at spiritual life today through the lens of people in mainstream religious congregations who have, heretofore, been largely invisible. However, for our purposes, an equally important part of these data is what it has to say about our own spiritual lives.

Part II is devoted to developing a point of view on how to use these data and their implications in your daily life which may enrich and expand the horizons of your *spiritual* life.

PART II
Giving The Gift Away!

6

A Point Of View And Three Observations

OK, so with all the data we've given you, why are we presenting you with a point of view and not a program? Why are we not turning this discussion into a series of "how to" statements that will guarantee your having a transformed life? The answer lies first with our data because they show there is no way to organize the experiences of our people into a programmatic scheme. Although people had essentially the same experience, there were as many ways of coming to that experience as there were people.

Second, the answer lies in the nature of programs themselves. Programs are an attempt to define and control a subject so that it can be more effectively manipulated. But in the case of spiritual programs, we're dealing with that which by nature cannot be defined or controlled. The more we try to define a spiritual program, the more we limit that which we are trying to define—in this case, God. Further, if our definition or program doesn't work for us, we feel that either we've failed or somehow the program failed which tends to make our participation in the program less desirable or successful.

Many spiritual programs are deductive in nature. They start with definitions and principles and reason their way to the individual and her/his activities. Our study started with individuals and in the gathering of data from them we moved from the individual to a general or universal statement of what these people experienced, which is an inductive approach.

Deductive programs tend to be limited by their assumptions. Inductive studies lead to generalizations from the data. This inductive approach helps to free one from preconceived notions and ideas of what ought to happen, and relies instead on what is observed or experienced.

What we are trying to say is that our people didn't follow a program to experience the presence or action of God in their lives. Their lives were simply interrupted by the presence or action of God; God became real to them and they were transformed. They knew it and they were absolutely clear about the source of their transformation even though they couldn't and didn't attempt to explain or define it.

We can't create that effect by behavioral changes that guarantee God's actions in our lives. (No ten steps to spiritual healing.) But we can see or observe the results of the presence or action of God. That's exactly what our collected stories do for us. They do not define God, but report on results of God's actions or presence. As we observe this trail of God's activity, we can develop a point of view which allows us to talk about the experience of transformation and to look for God in our own lives.

Based on our data, the following three observations form the initial basis for our point of view:

1. God is present and active in the world.

2. The activity of God in our study is a statistical reality and not an issue of faith alone.

3. There is a dimension to our lives which is legitimately called "spiritual" which differs qualitatively from the material or social dimension of our life (the world we live in) and has the power to transform it.

Let's look at each of these observations separately and see where they lead us.

1. God is present and active in the world.

Over 90% of the people we interviewed reported having a trans-forming experience of the presence or action of God in their lives. It is unlikely that we talked to the only three thousand people in the world who have had these experiences. Given the rich diver-sity of our sample and the range of experiences shared, it is not too much of a stretch to postulate that God is always present and active in the world. The real question is whether we will look at life as God present in each moment or not. If we do, then what we're saying is that every moment is a potentially transforming moment.

And that is exactly what we are proposing!

A transforming moment brings a new vision of reality to us. We operate from a new paradigm in which the old causalities and categories do not apply or are seen as different from what we previously thought or felt. The key to spiritual transforma-tion is to look at our life from the standpoint of God—real—and present in the moment, which can free us from the limitations of our usual ways of interpreting reality.

However, almost everything in life pushes us away from see-ing God in the moment. How can you rely on that which is unseen and out of our control? In fact, the more we feel we can control our lives, the less need we have for God, except on those occasions where we call upon God's power to help or save us in times of fear, desperation and/or helplessness.

In fact, in those times when we feel most in need, and least able to control our lives, we enter God's territory. Our ego may become temporarily mute and the mystery of God's presence can enter our consciousness as a new reality. At that moment, God becomes real and transformation can occur.

2. The activity of God in our study is a statistical reality and not an issue of faith alone.

The participants in our research were not talking about issues of faith in God present or active in the world. God *was* present and *real* to them. Data from the study give us this information in the form of statistical reality (numbers that can be measured) and not simply theological or faith assumptions.

In the usual language of religion, we talk about having "faith in God" even though we have no real idea of what God is and only a theological construct of what we think God should be. This requires us to believe or have faith that what we have constructed about God is true, as opposed to our experiencing God as real in our lives.

Our sample did not have to believe (have faith in) the presence of God in their life, they *knew* that God was present and active in their life through their direct experience with God. In speaking of that experience, they did not offer a definition of what God was. Instead they told us a story to help approximate what they knew or had experienced.

Experience "knows". That's why people told us stories and not theologies. Their experiences validated the presence of God, not the ambiguities of faith or belief. The numbers in our study quantify these experiences and provide a powerful picture of the extent of God's activity in the world that we studied.

3. There is a dimension to our lives which is legitimately called "spiritual", which differs qualitatively from the material or social dimension of our life (the world we live in) and has the power to transform it.

The stories that our people shared of the presence or action of God in their lives were of experiences clearly initiated by God, not themselves. Our population found, in the midst of living in the social and material world of our feelings, senses and intellect,

God suddenly entering into it, presenting an alternative experience of reality.

The descriptions of these events were free of the usual psycho/social explanations we employ about our experiences, often rooted in the past: e.g. this happened because my family was dysfunctional; or my father's drinking created all kinds of problems in my growing up. Instead we heard statements that were rooted in present time: "I suddenly felt God's arms around me"; or "I am so grateful for my disease".

These statements speak of a state best described as *spiritual* because people were talking about their experience of the presence or action of God in ways that were clear and unambiguous. People knew what they had experienced was true; but they did not attempt to explain it in any manner. Instead they chose to tell a story of the experience which opened the door to a reality beyond explanatory words.

Independent of their own actions or plans for the future, their lives were interrupted by what they were willing to call the presence or action of God. They weren't necessarily looking to find God. Instead, in some inexplicable way, God found them.

The spiritual dimension of life is a state in which we sense after something beyond ourselves and our ability to conceptualize, but that has a fundamental, undefined relationship with all of life. Our minds cannot possibly define God, the creative Mystery of the Universe. All our attempts to explain God only limit the limitless God.

Yet, there is something within us that sometimes knows there is more to life than what our senses and intellect provide. It hints at us in unexpected moments, or we sense its presence in situations that allow us to suddenly glimpse the existence of something other than ourselves and our reality.

Our sample entered into this spiritual dimension when they experienced the unexpected and real presence of God in their lives. This state defies rational explanations and suspends what we think of as cause and effect in the world. This causality is replaced by the Mystery of God Present, which is beyond our ability to describe, understand or control. The human necessity to explain what is going on breaks down in the face of this mystery.

In this sense, God present in every moment reflects a spiritual dimension in life which represents undefined and infinite possibilities, far beyond anything that we can define, predict or imagine.

In our limited material world, we search for methods of coping with what life puts into our path. But in our spiritual world, we enter into the mystery that can lead to new beginnings and transformation having little to do with our previous strategies and views of life. This is why we speak of God's Other Name as "surprise!"

It is essential to understand that transformation is a *spiritual* event. This is an important distinction because as human beings we are hard wired into having a "pay off" for our efforts. The gifts of the Spirit are spiritual, not material. They impact on the ordinary world through changes in our understanding of spiritual truth. The people in our study did not report that their external, material circumstances had necessarily changed for the "better", except in those situations in which people were physically cured of disease.

Instead, the interior world of the Spirit transforms the way people look at their life as it functions in the external world. These spiritual gifts are their own pay off because they have the power to transform experience itself and the way I evaluate my experiences.

We often see this phenomenon occurring when some event in life appears to be disastrous at first happening. Later we find it has opened the door to a deeper understanding or it turns out to be a gift in disguise which has transformed our lives.

One way of describing what happened to the people in our study is to say that they "opened their spiritual eyes" and in so doing they saw life as a new reality. And, in fact, reality can change to meet our measurements of it. That's the whole idea of the self-fulfilling prophesy.

But when we start to measure life with our "spiritual eyes" we find a different reality. Once this mode of seeing with our spiritual eyes becomes more habitual, the world of the spirit and the spiritual dimension of life come more into focus as a new way of viewing and interpreting our familiar material world.

The old familiar words, "I once was blind, but now I see; was lost but now am found" speak gently and profoundly about the process of seeing life with spiritual eyes. They are the simple testimony of a new spiritual reality and a transformed life.

7

On Seeing With Our Spiritual Eyes

Book stores are filled with books about spiritual paths and disciplines and ways to approach a spiritual life. Usually they offer a programmatic approach to achieving an increased state of spiritual awareness. But in our study we found only the mystery of the presence or action of God in people's lives and no specific program or plan that would achieve this state.

Instead, as noted in the previous chapter, we found a trail of God in the world told through the stories of people's experiences. Hearing these stories, and living with them these past thirteen years has certainly opened our spiritual eyes and provided us with a way in which one might look at the world through spiritual eyes.

It has allowed us to see how our data might apply to every day life, based on the three observations we talked about in the preceding chapter: (1) God is present and active in the world; (2) The activity of God in our study is a statistical reality and not a matter of faith alone; (3) There is a dimension to our lives which is legitimately called spiritual which differs qualitatively from the material dimension of life and has the power to transform it.

While it is clearly not within our power to understand the depth and mystery of God, we believe we can find some ways of thinking and being which will help us to be more receptive to God's presence.

In effect, we can look at any situation from two different points of view. One is our usual way of seeing the material world through our ego or "material" eyes which allows us to make judgments and create causalities with which we are all familiar. The other point of view allows us to look at what it might mean to see God in the moment and by so doing allow the possibility of the situation to be transformed into a new reality.

The first option allows us to stay where we are. The second option allows us to look at life through a spiritual lens and see where we could be.

Here's a way of organizing how we might do that. First, let's look at the way we ordinarily see the world with what might be called our "material eyes". Then we can see what it might be like to look at the world with our "spiritual eyes". This is the way it looks in a shorthand version.

OUR MATERIAL EYES	OUR SPIRITUAL EYES
1. Seeing material/social reality	Seeing the Presence & Action of God
2. Looking at my life with me as the "center"	Looking at my life with God as the "center"
3. Seeing life as problems needing solutions	Seeing life as opportunities and gifts
4. Looking for change	Finding transformation
5. Having expectations & goals	Finding surprises & the unexpected
6. Experiencing judgment, division & separation	Experiencing "oneness", wholeness & healing.
7. Asking, "What am I to do?"	Asking, "Where is God?"

We'll go through the chart expanding and commenting on each concept from both viewpoints. As we do that, try to put yourself into the chart to see where you are.

SEEING WITH OUR MATERIAL EYES:
1. SEEING MATERIAL/SOCIAL REALITY.

You know what it means to look at reality. It's what we see and experience everyday and what we know. No surprises or mystery here. But "seeing" is a lot more complicated than what we think or take for granted. What we see is also being filtered by our heart, experience and intellect and the limits of our own perception. In effect we create our own reality.

We are constantly judging and measuring what we experience, even though we may not be aware of the process. Our material eyes are also bound by time so that our understanding is affected by experiences from the past and hopes and dreams for the future.

Human behavior studies and psychology remind us that we are never operating within a simple process of "seeing", but rather are constantly engaged in the far more complex process of interpreting what we see. We judge things to be right or wrong, good or bad, appropriate or inappropriate which markedly influence the way we go about our daily living. This kind of filtering makes it possible for us to live in a complex, material world. We feel more comfortable because our filters put limits on the situation and make us feel we've taken control of it.

However, it is *our* picture of reality we are creating and it is not necessarily the same for others. Because we are talking about the same event or fact, we think we're all on the same page. But the meaning of each event or fact is highly individual. Our interpretation of the meanings other people hold does not necessarily coincide with their own personal reality. It is nearly impossible to fully know what is *real* to another person.

Fortunately, there is a generally agreed upon physical reality which allows us, for example, to drive down the street without our cars running into each other (most of the time). We all see the same red light and usually agree to stop for it. It is when we go beyond this kind of physical reality that we create our own picture of what reality is.

But within *our* measurement of reality, there is little room for God and the unexpected surprises of God. We're working too hard to simply maintain control, let alone deal with the mystery of God's *out of our control* appearances.

Now let's contrast this with how our spiritual eyes see reality.

SEEING WITH OUR SPIRITUAL EYES:
1. SEEING THE PRESENCE AND ACTION OF GOD.

Whereas our material eyes tend to look at a broad canvass of space and time, our spiritual eyes always look at the moment. Past and future do not exist in the spirit for God's presence is always *now*, not then or when, but in *this* particular moment. Our spiritual eyes cut across both time and history and their causalities as we understand them in our material world, and replace them with God present or acting in the moment. Immediately we are on a different playing field.

What our spiritual eyes reveal in the moment is infinite possibilities: the limitless God impacting our life, outside of our control or plan. This is the God of surprise and the unexpected moment that the people in our study described. Whereas our material eyes see a reality that is filtered by experience, social structures and what we want to see, our spiritual eyes see the certainty of God present without limitations. Our sample knew they had experienced the presence or action of God in the moment. This was the benchmark of their transformation and it was sufficient.

Seeing and recognizing the presence of God was the critical response. Most of the time we don't see God as present in the moment. Instead we default to our own explanations of what is happening in any given moment and hence erect a barrier to what God's presence might mean.

More often than not, we move out of the moment into the past or the future because we are time oriented. We have hopes, dreams and plans (or fears and dreads) about the future; we have happy or painful remembrances of the past. Or we are diverted by our immediate concerns in the present (e.g. I have a headache).

The biggest barrier to our recognizing the presence or action of God in our lives is our preconceived notion of what God is like and what God can/should do for us. It doesn't take much reflection to realize anything we could conceive in our minds as to the nature of God could come even close to the infinite mystery of what God actually is.

Seeing God in one's life transcends all preconceptions, ideas and expectations of what life should be and opens our future in ways we never dreamed possible. Following the trail of God, our sample always found that their transformation, when God became real, was more than and more wonderful than anything they could have conceived beforehand.

God's generosity is staggering and may take some getting used to.

SEEING WITH OUR MATERIAL EYES:
2. LOOKING AT MY LIFE WITH ME AT THE CENTER.

Our ways and attempts to organize our material and social world put us at the center of it, essentially making it our own creation. It is very easy then to see oneself as the center of our world, in which our life tasks are to bring success and happiness to ourselves and others through our efforts to exercise control and take charge.

Such behavior is certainly well attuned to the themes of independence under which we generally operate: "Take charge of your life"; "Be your own person"; "Be your own best friend". All these and other catch phrases of alleged freedom and independence are the principles on which we've been taught to survive and they represent high values in our society.

In fact, we are generally rewarded for our accomplishments and encouraged to work hard to be competent and independent in order to achieve the material rewards of success. That's the measurement of a well functioning individual in this material world. Anything less than that may be seen as somehow inadequate or weak.

Yet at the same time, being independent also separates us from others. To be the center of one's life means that we have to rely on ourselves in an increasingly complex world. Further, when we are the center of our life, it leaves little, if any, room for God.

In our competitive stance toward life, we may want to enlist God as our second in command in achieving our goals, acknowledging that having God (or God's power) on our side is probably the best of all possible worlds. But the mere idea of having God on our side keeps us in charge and robs God of the chance of being God.

Of course, the ultimate joke is that all our attempts to manage and control life, even with consummate skills and talents, are illusory. Unless you can control your next heart beat you don't control anything. But that doesn't stop us from trying.

SEEING WITH OUR SPIRITUAL EYES:
2. LOOKING AT MY LIFE WITH GOD AS THE CENTER.

The stories that our population told about their experiences were "God stories", that is God was clearly the center of the experience. These were stories that happened to the individual, but they were primarily about the unexpected arrival of God in the moment. For our population, God was the occupant of the center position. This understanding freed people from the limitations of their personal, psychological, historical, philosophical baggage, and the need to be number one, and replaced them with the infinite possibilities of God, the ultimate Center and Ground of Everything.

Time and again in many of the stories we heard, the locus of control was the central factor. If the control was with the individual, God was by and large blocked. When the locus of control was with God, the individual was able to be opened to the total experience and one's control became irrelevant.

It is our ability to see God as the Central fact of our life which allows us to let go of some of our need to control. However, relinquishing control is not an easy process for most of us. Control is hard wired into our being and has an infinite capacity to fool us into thinking that life revolves around us. Almost everything we learn about life leads us in that direction.

However, when we recognize the reality of God present and active in our world, in whatever way it happens, our ego may finally be able to be suspended—if only for a moment. That experience is the heart and spirit of transformation.

SEEING WITH OUR MATERIAL EYES: 3. SEEING LIFE AS PROBLEMS NEEDING SOLUTIONS.

When we are in charge of our life, the things that do not work out are seen as problems needing to be solved. Of course we want the solutions to be in our favor, consistent with our goals and desires. But we generally realize that some form of compromise may be needed to solve the problem in most social situations. So the role of compromise is usually translated into: how much can I win and/or how much must I lose?

The difficulty with this approach is that the solution to the problem is simply the redefinition of the problem. The initial problem still underlies the solution but the redefinition (usually negotiation) masks this reality. For instance, I want to go to my favorite restaurant, my wife wants to try another place. However we resolve that dilemma, there will be a residue of feeling which is left over from one of us not getting what we wanted in the first place.

Now if the new solution (redefinition) does not work out satis-factorily (the meal or the restaurant is not very good) the prob-lem is retrieved, old related issues are revisited ("you always get what *you* want") and the situation becomes increasingly complex and unsatisfactory.

Solutions, no matter how creatively crafted, are divisive at heart because both parties to some degree both win and lose in the compromise or redefinition. (You've probably heard this joke in one form or another: if you want to go to New York and I want to go to Chicago, we may compromise by finding ourselves in Cleveland!)

At the material or social level, life becomes a series of problem solving attempts to control or take charge of our lives. One of our most frequent strategies to *control* life is to explain or rationalize it and hope that our understanding will put limits on our prob-lems and thereby make us feel more comfortable. We frequently involve psychological explanations as a way of dealing with dif-ficult people or situations which can make us feel more in con-trol.

Yet, if we see life as a series of problems to be solved, our life will consist only of problems needing solutions. And when we get to that ultimate, unsolvable problem which is, of course, our death, then all bets are off!

SEEING WITH OUR SPIRITUAL EYES:
3. SEEING LIFE AS OPPORTUNITIES AND GIFTS.

As our social eyes see life as problems needing solutions, our spiritual eyes see life as situations containing opportunities and gifts. Seeing the situation as a gift is already a transforming expe-rience for the nature of gifts is to enrich our lives in a variety of ways. By taking a particular problem and redefining it as a spiri-tual gift, we automatically look for God in the process. That takes the edge off our trying to find a solution and refocuses our attention on the mystery of God present.

Spiritually, problems may be thought of as doorways into the world of the spirit: unexpected opportunities for us to look at "spiritual solutions" which are always gifts of transformation. The larger the problem, the more unsolvable it appears, the greater opportunity we have to challenge and look beyond our usual ways of problem solving to at least acknowledge our inadequacy and helplessness in order to make room for the discovery of God present in the heart of any situation.

As with all the surprises of God, the solution is to see these problems or conflicts as potential gifts, *not caused by God*, but situations in which God may be found. We can then focus on the contents of the gift, God present and acting, and the possibility of transformation expressed within what we are calling a problem.

Now, in the material world, problems do not go away simply because we are able to look at them as spiritual gifts. What *can* happen is that the insights of a spiritual gift may allow us to come back to what we have perceived as a problem and find a different way to deal with it.

In other words, the "head to head" that we are experiencing with our teenager may be transformed into a question of how do we love each other in the mutual process of entering a new stage of life with each other, (in which there are gains and losses for both parties), not how we can control the situation and remain in charge. Converting a problem to a question reflects the transforming nature of Spirit in action. A question can have an answer. A problem can only have a redefinition.

A gift is also a mystery over which we have no control. What God is offering is the gift of God present in this particular moment. When God is the Giver, we can expect abundant surprises and fulfillment beyond our imaginings. But remember! These are *spiritual* gifts and they may differ markedly from our expectations associated with our material gift giving and receiving.

Spiritual Gifts can "knock your socks off"—they can turn your life upside down or inside out. After all, they are the Gifts of a Creator God who knows none of our limitations. They have within them the possibility of transforming the material world because they do not share the same limited goals as finding solutions to a problem. Receiving a gift is a totally different experience from having a problem.

Our people did not report that their problems were suddenly solved or that life had become blissful or trouble free. In many instances, the problems remained the same, *but the people were different*. Spiritual gifts are not designed to give you pleasure as are material gifts. Instead, they offer the infinite possibilities of new life and transformation which is the ultimate gift we can receive.

SEEING WITH OUR MATERIAL EYES:
4. LOOKING FOR CHANGE.

So we go through life, trying to be responsible and manage our own affairs with some degree of skill and persistence. Generally speaking our goal is to alter or change the world around us to fit more into what we want or what we think it ought to be. Change is a kind of hope for the future that things can and will get better and is generally seen as good, healthy and inevitable in this life. If you don't change then you're staying the same. Being stuck in a changeless state means you can't move ahead in this world. That's clearly not the way we should be living our lives.

In our search for change, what we envision the world ought to be is a function of our special view of reality. Inasmuch as other people might not share that view, then change also can create divisions between us. Your change may impinge on my life in a way I don't want or approve. My change may be costly to your standards of living. Change does not operate in a vacuum. Once set in motion, there are always unexpected consequences that can turn around and bite us.

Our yearning for change has deep roots. We sense the unsatis-factory-ness of life and hope that in doing something different we may find some peace. Or we make a change and hope it will distract us from some unhappiness in our life. But change for change sake only reveals the depth of our dissatisfactions. The quick fix or the geographic cure can turn out to be short cuts to our own emptiness.

There are certain areas in which change does accomplish something. You clean up the water supply and people don't get sick from dysentery. However the consequences of putting in a water treatment plant in a given area may in itself change things in ways we can't predict. And so our changes have built in uncertainties and unexpected results.

Some changes we would define as *good* changes. Others we would describe as *bad* changes, for not all change is considered desirable. But changes occur all the time whether we want them to or not.

Our physical world changes, our physical bodies change and we have a limited ability to slow down or alter these kinds of changes. People change; fashions change; politics change; rules change. However, in terms of the way we are forced to deal with change as human beings, the old proverb probably does apply: "the more things change, the more they stay the same".

In spite of the increasing number of changes occurring in our lives and in the world, we are often hard pressed to see how things are different or better. Change is a slippery slope. Mostly we try to keep up with the changes and hope for the best.

SEEING WITH OUR SPIRITUAL EYES:
4. FINDING TRANSFORMATION.

Change is to transformation as going steady is to marriage. They look a lot alike, but there are fundamental differences between them. We change our clothes, our jobs, our homes; we change our minds, our plans and our new year's resolutions, but we remain the same us. However, transformation is a change of state. When God becomes *real* to us, we don't remain the same us. Something is different that is perceptible though not necessarily visible. And life is never quite the same.

Transformation changes our *being*. Our attempts to control life are replaced with the results of our experience of God present or acting. This frees us from the restrictions and impediments of our self limitations and allows us to be opened to new and unexpected possibilities.

Our sample reported benchmarks or pivotal moments when their lives were transformed, made different by the experience of the presence or action of God. In the process of transformation, we are made over in the image of God. This does not mean that we become "God". But it does mean that when we have experienced the reality of God, we now become God's agents: the voice and actions of God's presence in the world.

Stated another way, we have received a gift which must be shared. And that's precisely what happened to the people in our study, as they described the quality of their lives after their experiences of the presence or action of God.

SEEING WITH OUR MATERIAL EYES:
5. HAVING EXPECTATIONS AND GOALS.

Human beings have a basically creative nature which makes us ask "What if?" or "How could that be?" This creativity carries with it the expectations that life could be made better and problems could be eliminated which leads us to create goals to accomplish our dreams. Although this goal setting may be commendable, the uncertainty that lies within the nature of life makes the realization of many of our goals difficult at best.

Even when we realize a goal, we cannot begin to comprehend the complexities that lie within this new state. Even the most sophisticated planning is hard pressed to recognize or control all the possibilities. In this sense, our planning and goal setting in life is often a "crap shoot". Sometimes we come up with a winner, sometimes we don't.

Further, there is a randomness which operates in spite of our best efforts which can alter even the best laid plans. The principle might be stated: the larger and more complex the goal, the less predictable the effects of achieving the goal will be.

In having expectations and setting goals, there is one unknown that we cannot account for besides the unpredictable outcomes of chance or luck. That, of course, is the Mystery of God acting in the world, which is why we generally leave God, chance and luck out of our goal setting.

On the other side of the coin, when we do include God in our goal setting, it may be because we believe God is on our side and therefore the goal is right and brooks no opposition. We expect God's power to protect us, overcome our enemies and give us what we want. The proper name for that activity is idolatry.

In either case, we're still the ones in charge and God is relegated to the back seat.

SEEING WITH OUR SPIRITUAL EYES:
5. FINDING SURPRISES AND THE UNEXPECTED.

The stories people told us were not about goal oriented plans for the future. God was always the great surpriser! Not only was the unexpected presence of God generally a surprise, the outcome of the experience turned out to be a surprise as well.

However, that shouldn't be a surprise to us. In the spiritual dimension of life God is in charge, not us. That which is seen with our spiritual eyes differs markedly from the way we organize our social/material world. As such, our limited goals and expectations don't even come close to the generosity of God's gifts.

People reported that the outcome of their experience with God was always more than what they had planned or expected. We see ourselves as individuals with needs and desires; God sees us as part of God's creation. We see life with limited eyes; God introduces an unlimited playing field. As we are caught in a two dimensional universe of cause and effect, God breaks through like a modern day Gabriel bringing us good tidings of great joy.

We are like captives in the prison of our own material world and understanding. Let God loose in our lives and all the walls break down. When we talk about God in our own material/ social world, we tend to make God in our own limited image. But when we *experience* God, we are a part of God's infinite possibilities where everything is a surprise and an unexpected gift to all.

When you come right down to the bottom line, you have to remember that God's other name has always been *Surprise!* So, the moral of this story is: always be prepared to be surprised and see what happens next.

SEEING WITH OUR MATERIAL EYES:
6. EXPERIENCING JUDGMENT, DIVISION AND SEPARATION.

Underlying our whole structure of reality is a series of judgments we make about its nature. Just think for a moment how we determine whether something is true or not. Any statement can be declared true only if we know for certain that it is not false. "This is my car" is a true statement if we can produce ownership papers. If the ownership papers have a different name on them, it's a false statement.

Our judgments are inherently divisive in that we look to the opposite pole of the judgment to determine our own truths. We know what is "good" because we have decided what is "bad". We understand what is "right", because we have determined what is "wrong". As human beings, we operate in a judgmental system which is highly limiting.

The positive side of judgment and division is that it allows us to process what comes at us in this world with relative efficiency and makes our life less complicated and more secure. The sum of our judgments establishes our positions in life. Although being sure of my positions may bring me more peace of mind, it also limits my tolerance of the positions of others.

The down side of judgment and division *fixes*, that is places, other people in a given context and separates us from them. "Unless you're for me, you're against me" is the defining mechanism of separation. Our judgments about life, however well meaning, separate us from others. Further, it puts others into our definition of who they are and removes their freedom to change our view of them. We have decided who they are and closed our eyes to any other evidence. This is the basis of prejudice and it creates untold chaos in our material/social life.

Society is organized on the basis of judgment and division. It makes laws which include or exclude people and their behaviors. The problem with this is that it creates people on either side of a situation as separate and possibly in conflict with each other. This is the nature of social structures which speak of the "common good" and then divides us into opposingcategories of us and them.

In reality, we *are* separate individuals. But in seeing ourselves as separate from others, we may also see ourselves as separate from that Creative Mystery we call God. The separation we feel from God is a product of our incessant struggle to survive in a world in which we frequently feel alone, left to our own survival devices. Fortunately God is not limited by our system of reality.

SEEING WITH OUR SPIRITUAL EYES:
6. EXPERIENCING ONENESS, WHOLENESS AND HEALING.

The amazing thing about the spiritual state is that contrary to our material experiences, it is unipolar, not bi-polar. God present and active in the moment has no opposite for there is never a moment when God is not present and active, by definition.

Our spiritual eyes see the reality of wholeness, oneness and healing in every moment. Without exception, all the stories in our study contained this reality as the underlying theme of each story. In a particular moment, people described the healing presence or action of God. Within that experience, there was no separation between God and the individual, only oneness and connection.

We have a peculiar problem as human beings. Our ego is that which distinguishes us from others. But at the same time, it separates us from them as well and it is this powerful sense of separation which underlies much of our dissatisfaction and despair about the world and our place in it.

When we experience the presence or action of God in our lives, we feel a sense of reunion which we describe as an experience of peace, the peace that "passes all understanding". In that experience of reunion, separation is overcome and we see the oneness of ourselves, others and God.

In the material world, we long for reunion. In the spiritual world, we find that we have never been separated.

SEEING WITH OUR MATERIAL EYES:
7. ASKING, "WHAT AM I TO DO?"

We've been talking about the way we function in our social/material world. Our role as the center of our lives, our desire for solutions and change, our expectations, judgments, setting goals and looking for results and success all come down, finally, to us, the ultimate bottom line. Inevitably, they lead to one single question in regard to our lives: "What am I to do?"

This is the question which reveals the essential nature of our struggle: the *I* that is separate from others; the *action* that I must take to make things right; and the *what* of not knowing what in the world that might be. All these speak of our separation, even in the midst of other people. The basic syntax of our lives is one of separation. Even in our religious language, we speak of an I/Thou relationship with God which is the essence of separation. Separation is hard-wired into our being.

In fact, our earliest experience with life is the separation from the maternal source that carried and nourished us. Our growth into adulthood and throughout life is a continuous process of differentiating ourselves from all others. Even in our intimate relationships, we speak of maintaining our boundaries to ensure that we continue to be our own person. The question, "What am I to do", is the persistent question of a differentiated state of being, struggling alone to control life.

Fortunately, there is another question to ask.

SEEING WITH OUR SPIRITUAL EYES:
7. ASKING, "WHERE IS GOD?"

Because our spiritual eyes are built to see God in the material world around us, the spiritual question paired with "What am I to do?" becomes, "Where is God in this moment?" This is by nature a transforming question because it moves us into the spiritual world where God's presence is known. This question gives us the chance to look at our material life in a new way, if we will take it.

All the ways we've described the world as seen through our spiritual eyes: experiencing God as real in my life; seeing life with God as the center; seeing life as opportunities and gifts; finding transformation, surprises and the unexpected; experiencing oneness, wholeness and healing all lead us to raise this question as the key to spiritual life. We ask, "Where is God in this moment" with the expectation and knowledge that God is precisely here. That understanding changes everything.

When we ask, "Where is God in this moment?", we automatically open the door to the "spiritual world" and behind that door is always our old friend, "Surprise!"

Take a moment or two to look at this chart again and see where you find yourself in the process now.

OUR MATERIAL EYES	OUR SPIRITUAL EYES
1. Seeing material reality	Seeing the Presence & Action of God
2. Looking at my life with me as the "center"	Looking at my life with God as the "center"
3. Seeing life as problems needing solutions	Seeing life as opportunities & gifts.
4. Looking for change	Finding transformation
5. Having expectations & goals	Finding surprises & the unexpected
6. Experiencing judgment, division & separation	Experiencing "oneness", wholeness, & healing
7. Asking, "What am I to do?"	Asking, "Where is God?"

One could easily look for other pairings in this schematic look at our material vs. spiritual eyes. Much of our lives are spent in **looking for the results** of our efforts, the tangible evidence of life and work at a level of pleasure and competency. Good results produce satisfaction; bad results give us a sense of failure or inadequacy.

And yet, the spiritual pairing takes the issue of results and lifts up the task of **finding meaning** in life. Meaning transcends our result oriented existence and shows us a measurement of life not available in the black and white limitations of results and bottom lines.

In a similar fashion, one might talk about our preoccupation with **seeking success** in our material world in the myriad ways in which we define success. However, we immediately run up against the ephemeral nature of success. Today's success can be converted into tomorrow's failure as easily as the stock market can change directions. Success is not static, but rises and falls at the whims of an uncaring society. Today's super hero is entirely dependant upon a public that follows where the wind blows, sometimes with no visible or apparent reason.

When one can transpose our need to be successful into its spiritual counterpart, **the discovery of new life,** we enter a world in which God becomes the creator of that new life. We are free to enter it or not. But the substance it contains is the constancy of God and not the fickle nature of success. A far more reliable choice.

Obviously we can and do move back and forth between the material and spiritual all the time. But when we move from our material eyes to our spiritual eyes, we have the possibility of leaving our social baggage behind and transforming it into something else. That something else will always be more than we could possibly have imagined it to be.

If you will, the dynamic movement between these two states opens us to receive the gift of transformation.

Asking the question, "Where is God in this moment?" is the critical question that can open the door to knowing the real presence of God in our life. Like a flashing red light, it stops our perpetual motion, breaks into our automatic behaviors, and acknowledges the existence of that Transcendent Creative Mystery which makes all things new.

8

The Critical Years

Our data produced one more unexpected, and highly significant, surprise having to do with the ages at which people reported experiences of the Presence or Action of God. We looked particularly at the age range between the onset of these experiences and the age at which they appeared to diminish or disappear. Graphs can sometimes give us a picture that words cannot quite describe, or describe in less colorful ways. So first, let's show you the graph. Then we'll talk about what it has to tell us.

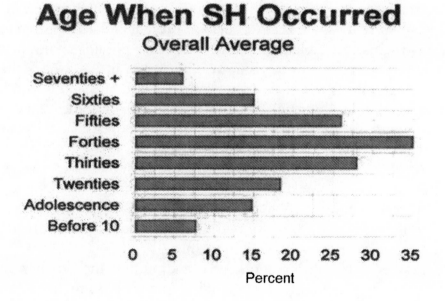

Age When SH Occurred
Overall Average

The first thing you'll see is that 35% of our sample reported experiences of the presence or action of God in their 40's. This was the peak time for these experiences. The 30's were the next most fertile period and the 50's followed close behind. So what you're seeing is that the years between 30 and 59 accounted for 89% of the reported experiences.

These are what we are calling "The Critical Years", those years in which God's presence and action were described as occurring most often.

What interested us was the fact that these are also the years in which people are most engaged in the material world of career, family, achievement, and the establishment of place in the world. These are the years in which we struggle to "make it" and climb to the peak of our potential. They are also the complicated years of family and marital struggles; problems with aging parents; financial pressures; the beginning of health concerns and mid life crises. (By previous observation, a fertile field for God.)

It is clear that if you are within this age group (30-59), you are especially vulnerable and open to a spiritual orientation toward life, because these experiences of God present and active seem to be particularly visible in this time frame. We are not saying that such experiences do not occur at other times in life. Check the chart again to note the activity in our 20's and 60's and beyond. But there is an undeniable trend toward these middle years of adulthood as critical times of transforming experiences in your life.

As you have seen from our stories and data, these experiences are not unusual, once in a lifetime, miraculous, mountain top occurrences in people's lives. Rather they are the stuff of every-day life experience, transformed in the moment by recognizing the presence or action of God in them.

However, transformation needs tending and the problem in this age range is that we are attending to multiple situations and demands. These years have become overwhelming in their pressures on individuals and families. Bills have to be paid; the family has to be fed. Our social and family obligations seem to compound in ways that often feel out of control. It has become a time with literally no time out available.

It is relatively easy, if we're not careful, to park these spiritual experiences in a closet of off-season clothes and not give them the imperative which they contain. We don't forget exactly; we just don't remember very well.

Worse yet, we fail to share them with others so that the gift is lost and not returned into the relational world of family, friends, coworkers, neighbors and the world at large. Spiritual sharing is difficult in our society and not part of our usual social interactions. Most people simply don't talk about God as an everyday part of life. Even our mainstream, institutional religious life does not necessarily include talking about one's personal experience of God in that environment.

Yet the profound truth about spiritual gifts is they survive and grow by being shared. When people are willing to take a chance and talk about God, the gifts of transformation become available as unexpected, new life possibilities. It doesn't take much to introduce the subject of God into a moment of time. A simple statement about the spiritual component of this moment and we are already engaged in a conversation about God.

Acknowledging the presence of God within any given situation automatically changes the experience. Try it—you may be surprised at the effect it produces. It can create a momentary space or opening for Spirit to enter the scene, giving us a chance to catch our breath and shift our vision toward a different reality. It can expand the situation, if only for a millisecond of actual time, but with the potential for infinite time.

The opportunities for talking about God in these middle life, critical years are endless. In our intimate relationships, the feeding of our mutual *spiritual* needs is rarely considered. We're simply too busy with all of life's other demands. Yet the experience of spiritual intimacy, the sharing of the gifts of the presence or action of God, is a powerful means of nurturing the relationship. In fact, this is true of any relationship. Introduce the sharing of spiritual experiences and you may just transform the relationship.

Now remember! Don't ask if this will *improve* the relationship. That plus/minus dimension is the wrong direction. Look for transformation and new life—even if that new life leads your relationship into a place that may initially be uncomfortable or unfamiliar. Go with God and see what happens. The odds are heavily in your favor to experience a new dimension of intimacy.

The family is a dominant force in these middle years. If one learns to talk about God within the family, that knowledge is more easily expanded into the world because it is part of the life-learning that occurs within the years of living at home. It's like a base camp of God Present and Active, providing the equipment to allow us to move out into the world.

We are not suggesting you add one more item to your already over programmed family life. But we are proposing that in simple, unstructured ways, one can talk about God as easily as one talks about the food we eat or the television program we're watching or the myriad of events that combine to create our family. We could decide to become the family that talks about God as part of its identity and see what happens.

In the broader social environment in which these middle adult years are spent, an openness to exploring the mutual presence or action of God can lead us to wholeness rather than division. Each of these explorations represent opportunities to talk about situations that need tending, not in terms of right or wrong, but in the much larger picture of God's transformational presence. The question "Where is God in *this* situation" is the one question guaranteed to bring alternative possibilities into a situation that appears to contain troubling or irreconcilable differences.

In the market place, some companies are already learning the value of time spent in prayer and spiritual conversation in the transformation of the whole work environment. It has increased both production and morale.

In fact, there is no situation in our life that does not benefit from being able to look at it with our spiritual eyes to see possibilities for transformation that exist within it. But we must be willing to take the spiritual chance at the time we are presented with it.

As one of our stories reminds us, "*I was driving a friend home one night when she told me of a very painful thing in her life. I listened and then I stopped the car and took her hand. My friend said, 'we can go on now' and I might have just done that. Ordinarily I would have. But instead I said, 'we should pray'. I somehow knew that she wanted to pray too, but that's a hard thing to ask people to do. Having said what I did, I didn't really know what to say. But I thought of the verse, 'Be still and know that I am God'. I don't know why ... it just came into my head. But after that, it was easy. That started it. God was there.*"

One of the things we noted in our data gathering was how hungry people were to both tell their stories and to hear the stories that others had to tell. You may be surprised at how acceptable your spiritual conversation can be with acquaintances and even good friends and family. Take a chance and see what happens.

Talking about God in our lives is a kind of universal solvent which breaks us loose from our locked in, unyielding materialistic world and opens the way for us to acknowledge who we really are: the beloved children of God, part of the transforming Mystery of the Universe. What that means can only be translated through the stories we share of our spiritual experiences and our actions in life as a result of them.

Our middle years carry one more imperative. Arbitrarily these critical years end at age sixty which is now designated as the beginning of old age. If we live to be 90 years of age, thirty percent of our lives will be lived in old age and this is being extended all the time. However, the ground work for a transforming spiritual old age is laid in those critical years between the ages of thirty and fifty-nine. In fact, these experiences of the presence or action of God in our middle years become even more important in old age as a counter balance to the inevitable uncontrollable experiences of the aging process.

These out-of-our-control aspects of aging are powerful and unavoidable. Issues of our health, emotional and mental stability, the loss of friends and family, the question of financial security lead us eventually to the increasing awareness of our death. Each of these issues can become overwhelming without a spiritual anchor on which to stand. As one chaplain in a retirement home told us, "If you don't prepare *spiritually* for your old age when you are in your thirties, you'll never make it".

Our current population of baby boomers (born between 1946 and 1964) are square in the middle of these critical years and are just now entering their old age. For those "boomers" who would like to find continuing growth and satisfactions in the aging process, it is essential they develop their spiritual lives within the time frame when Spirit is so potentially available. On that foundation is laid the path toward a transformed old age.

These middle years of life, filled to overflowing with the material tasks of living, represent the achievement of independence and the mastery of a multitude of life tasks. They are the bridge between childhood and old age. These are also the years, it would seem, when God appears on the scene with greater frequency and intensity. In the midst of time packed full of responsibilities and challenges, God surprises us with the spiritual dimension of life and gives us the opportunity to open our spiritual eyes, not as another task but as an opportunity to see beyond the overload of being "too busy".

This God of every-present-moment enters into the very heart and center of our life in its most preoccupied state and offers us not only the gift of transformation but also the gift of simplification. Looking for God in the moment simplifies our life by substituting one measurement for all of the other countless ones we use to control our lives and has the ability to transform them in ways that are always surprising and healing.

Remember: Our data show this to be true for everyone at any stage in life. The frequency may be greater for those between the ages of 30 and 59 but it is by no means limited to those ages. The important message at any age is to be open to the spiritual nature of life as reflected in the question, "Where is God in this moment?"

And the answer to that question will always be ageless!

9

Two More Observations—One Critical Question!

So here we are at an interesting fork in the road. We've given you data from our study which covers the stories of over three thousand people who reported having experienced the presence or action of God in their lives. We've told you their words and stories and provided that wonderful array of statistical evidence that points toward the universality of God's presence in life. We've offered you three observations about spiritual life.

Now comes the moment of truth. You can say, "that was interesting ..." close the book and continue your life as is. Or, you can say, "Well, I really want to find out what's at the end of this path. So, what's next?"

What's next? We're going to follow God's surprises in the lives of five people in ways which are powerful and transforming and then try to persuade you to take a chance on God and discover some God surprises and spiritual truths in your life.

We'll tell you two stories and look at them from the standpoint of seeing with our material eyes and seeing with our spiritual eyes and look at the difference.

"We had been camping for about three weeks and I needed to go into town to get some things. My son wanted to go along and when we got there—it was a terribly hot day—he said that he didn't want to go to the store with me. And he didn't want to sit in the car and wait for me. What he wanted to do was to go down into the park by the river. I thought about it and then said to him, 'OK, but be careful'.

When I finished shopping and started back to my car, some boys came up and said that my son had gone into the river and was swept over the falls. I was frantic and very frightened. I wanted to pray but realized that God couldn't undo what was already done. I thought maybe it was someone else ... somebody else's son going over the falls. All the things that go through your head when you're desperate.

Then I had a sense of God's arms around me. I knew I would survive in God's love ... even if the worse had happened ... if my son had died. I said, 'So that's what God's love is all about ... that's what it means.' And I felt so peaceful. It was amazing.

When I got to the hospital, I found that my son was hurt, but not badly hurt and that he would be OK. It was a transforming experience for me."

If we look at this story with our social/material eyes, one way of seeing it is that the woman was focused on herself, "I knew *I* would survive in God's love ... even if the worst happened ... if my son had died". It might sound as if all she cared about was her own survival.

But that's only because we insist on certain ways of evaluating life and expect God to comply with our value system.

It is clear from the story that God was present to the woman in a way that was different from what we expected to hear. The powerful spiritual truth she told us was about God's loving presence which can transcend any situation within the material world. "I felt God's arms around me ... I felt so peaceful ... it was amazing".

Most parents would agree that losing a child is about the worst thing that can happen in life. But what this woman experienced in her story was the loving presence of God which transformed the situation from loss and terror into an experience of peace, regardless of the outcome.

In other words, God's presence *was* the transformation. Having envisioned the worst that could happen, she also discovered a new meaning of God's love. "So that's what God's love is all about". The fact of her son's deliverance from serious injury or death was another issue.

It's important to note that the woman didn't ask God to save her child. "I wanted to pray but realized that God couldn't undo what had already been done". But in the midst of her fears and guilt, suddenly God's presence revealed itself in the way she described, transforming the entire experience into a revelation of God's love.

Ordinarily in circumstances such as these, we would have expected the mother to desperately pray for her son's safety, and frantically hope that God would grant her request.

This interpretation would have limited God's presence or action to answering a deeply heartfelt prayer which is a very human view of what God ought to do. However, defining what God *should do* is highly limiting to what God actually is.

Instead she experienced the presence of God and the peace of God's love and she understood the unlimited nature of God, even before she learned of her son's safety.

The fact that she was so "amazed" by the experience demonstrates just how different spiritual truth is from the limitations of human understanding. Ordinary interpretations of this event would include our gratitude and relief. Spiritual truths take us to a new place and our lives are never the same again. This is the hallmark of transformation.

When we told this story to a group at Oxford University in England, one of the women in the audience began to cry as I shared the words, "And I felt God's arms around me and I knew I would survive in God's love, even if the worst happened". The story she shared involved a situation in which she was a bank clerk who was a victim of a robbery at the bank. All the employees were tied up, blind folded and forced to sit along a wall, while the armed robbers set about their work. In the midst of her terror, she also had felt "God's arms around her and she knew somehow she would be OK".

It was as if the first story had the power to recreate the experience of the second story.

A wordless, profound connection was formed between two women who lived across the ocean from each other but who each had remarkably similar experiences of the transforming power of God's presence.

Let's take another story, one in which the authors were involved.

"We had put in a long day and pulled into the parking lot of the Holiday Inn about midnight. You know when you get to any motel at midnight ... not only are you exhausted ... but nothing else seems to work right. Finally we fell into bed around 2:00 a.m., knowing we had to be up at 6:00 a.m. because we had to drive across the state of Pennsylvania to visit our next church. It was exhausting just thinking about it.

After fitfully sleeping the few hours we had, I woke Lew a little before 6:00 a.m. I had noticed that the restaurant was open at 6:00. I thought maybe most people would arrive later and we could get in and out quickly. We dressed in a hurry and arrived at the restaurant by 6:15, only to find about a dozen other people with the same idea. 'Oh well,' I thought, 'we'll still get out in time ... it will work out.'

But it didn't quite turn out that way. It seemed the cook and waitress hadn't arrived either. So we all waited. Finally they showed up, and hope returned. But it turned out that we were the last people the waitress waited on. By that time, I was annoyed and frustrated. We ate eggs that seemed cold, just like the coffee, and left as soon as we finished.

The layout of the Holiday Inn is important for this story. The restaurant is at the far east end and the parking lot at the opposite west end. To get to the parking lot, you have to pass the lobby desk, and go through a corridor to the west exit. And to get to our van, you had to go to the furthest western corner of the parking lot. That's what happens when you're the last person to arrive at the motel.

We got into our van, Lew had just turned on the key to the ignition when we heard a knock at the door. There stood the waitress and she was carrying ... my purse!! In our haste to leave, I had left it at the restau-

rant. But the thing that I noticed even more than my purse was the look of concern on the face of the waitress. All my frustration melted in the face of such caring.

I stammered something that sounded like 'Thanks so much' ... and then said quietly to Lew, 'Give me some money, I want to give her a tip'. But hearing my words, she responded, 'I don't want a tip ... I want you to have what you need!' I took my purse from her, thanking her again and slowly closed the door.

As I watched her walk away, I realized that because of the particular layout of the Holiday Inn, she had to have literally run from the restaurant to our van to stop our leaving ... I also realized that she could have left my purse in the restaurant (after all I had been pretty crabby about having to wait and the slow service); she could have dropped it off at the front desk—much easier. But she brought it directly to us, making sure we had it before we left.

Then we drove in silence for what seemed like about 100 miles. Then I suddenly realized what had happened ... 'Lew', I said, ... 'Lew, that was God ... bringing me what I need ... making sure that I actually received the gift ... not wanting a tip ... just wanting to give me what was necessary for my life'. I paused, realizing what an incredible, unbelievable experience we had just had. This is exactly what God is ... what God does ... caring about us, chasing after us, trying to give us what we need ... going beyond all limits to make sure that we receive the gift ... and knowing exactly what gift we need."

This is certainly a story about some of the frustrations of living in the material world. We were in a hurry and concerned only with our agenda. We had made a judgment about who the waitress was and what kind of job she was doing. It was not a very complimentary assessment. In fact our reality at that time had condensed into one state of annoyance and frustration where nothing seemed to be going right.

The interruption of our departure by the waitress knocking on the door of the van was a total surprise. She was certainly the last person we expected to see and just as certainly we were not prepared to discover God in any part of this situation. And yet, in her simple concern that "I get what I need", it became absolutely clear that God was also present in the van at that moment. When we recognized that spiritual truth, life was transformed for us.

My words, "Lew, that was God" created a deep spiritual connection with God. However, the gift in this situation was not the return of the lost purse. Rather it was the gift of the return of two, tired, "lost sheep" who had lost their way in the world of frustration and material demands (which is to be lost indeed) and who were found by a loving, active Creator God living in the heart of a waitress.

These two stories show how different seeing with our spiritual eyes can be from seeing with our material eyes which are limited to our rather tiny view of reality. Out of our spiritual eyes come spiritual truths. When we recognize God's presence in the present moment, these truths can enter our lives and transform them.

Now we can add a fourth and fifth observation to our list. But first, let's restate the original three in their simplest terms:**God is here; God is real; God is now.**

Our collected stories certainly illustrate the experienced presence and activity of God in the world and the discovered existence of a spiritual dimension which has the power to transform our material world. These data validate the statistical reality of these experiences.

The fourth observation might be stated:

4.   **Transformation begins with the acknowledgment of the presence or action of God in the actual moment.**

Everything we've said throughout this book is an illustration of our fourth observation.

In the moment of transformation, time collapses into the present moment and past and future cease to exist. As a result we are freed from both these constraints of time which so power-fully influence our material lives.

For *that moment*, our usual causality is suspended and God's infinitely possible creativity is all that exists. This is a moment of total freedom while, paradoxically, it is also a moment of being absolutely claimed by God.

It doesn't take a pivotal spiritual experience in order to under-stand the essential truth embedded in the question, "Where is God in the moment?" We can take this concept of God present in the moment and use it as a new way of measuring how we per-ceive what is going on in our life.

This allows us to look at experience in a different way. We are not *creating* God in the moment, we are taking a chance on God's *being* in the moment which allows us to open our eyes and expe-rience to a different way of looking at things. It is the difference between *seeing* with our material eyes and *opening* our spiritual eyes, as we talked about in the last chapter.

When we look at life through the filters we ordinarily use to interpret our experience, life shows us what we expect to find. But these filters can change and life will respond to that change and help us to create a new reality. This is the essence of what religion calls "conversion".

However we choose to measure our experiences, life will oblige our persistence. In choosing to be sensitized to the pres-ence of God in our lives, we automatically begin to pay closer attention to the possibilities of God in the moment. In fact, as we start to look for God, we always see more of God.

This is not to say, or imply, that God or God's presence is in any way a product of our imagination or intellect. Our data show that the experience of God's presence is iconoclastic, breaking apart our preconceptions of how things ought to be. Even the people who have had these experiences cannot tell us precisely what the experience means, but they can tell us a story about the experience, and through that story tell us something about the transforming nature of God.

We don't have words to describe what God is, much less explain God's presence or action. But we can consciously view life through the question, "Where is God in this moment" which allows us the possibility of transcending our own human limitations and look for that which has not been apparent before. We are free to experience God's reality as different from ours because the locus of control has now shifted from us to God (a theme we found throughout our study). We can re-measure our life through this critical question because the measuring tape is God's, not ours.

The fifth observation is:

5.   **Having received the gift of God's presence, we are under an obligation to share it.**

This observation takes the question, "Where is God in this moment?" and moves us directly back into life where we become the expression of God's answer in the material world. We take the gift and return it into the world where it can be received by others.

In effect, we become "obedient" to our obligation to share the gift of God's presence. The lovely and unexpected surprise of our Fifth Observation is that contrary to being experienced as an obligatory burden, the nature of spiritual gifts is such that to give them away only increases the gift both to us and to the receiver.

Giving these gifts to others has two critical components: The first is to share your story of the presence or action of God in your life. The second is to look for some active way to express your experience in the world. Be advised: *to not share the gift is to lose the opportunity to reflect God's Presence in the world.*

Gifts are always symbols of relationships. So the gift of God's presence both relates us to God and impels us to move into the world of others with the gifts we have received from God. Ordinarily, if you give a gift away, you no longer have it. When you give away a spiritual gift to another, now two people have the gift and the gift is doubled.

This process is not an ego trip nor a method of aggrandizing ourselves but a mission and adventure into tracking the active Spirit of God present in every moment. If it becomes an ego trip, then we've become God-like instead of God-gifted and we have moved back into the material world where we are the center and God is on the periphery.

As we see more clearly with our "spiritual eyes", life automatically becomes an ongoing cycle of receiving and returning the gifts of God's presence.

So let's take a look at all five observations together:

1. **God is present and active in the world.**

2. **This activity of God in our study is a statistical reality and not an issue of faith alone.**

3. **There is a dimension to our lives which is legitimately called "spiritual" and which differs qualitatively from the material and has the power to transform it.**

4. **Transformation begins with the acknowledgement of the presence of God in the moment.**

5. **Having received the gift of God's presence we have an obligation to share it.**

These observations point us in a direction that transcends our ordinary ways of thinking about life and moves us into a brand new landscape with God in the center. In the language of today, God is present 24/7 and we have the opportunity to experience God's Presence at any time. God is always open for "business".

Earlier in this book, we've talked about the profound effect asking the right question can have on your life. The critical question, "Where is God in this moment?" is the doorway into the world of the Spirit. So hang on to this question because it's like no other question you will ever ask. Ask it in *any situation* ... ask it *in every situation* ... and the seeds of transformation will be present.

Now some would say that it's very difficult to look at life and see terrible things happening and then declare that God is present in every moment. Yet that is exactly what the people in our study told us repeatedly. In the most extreme and tragic situations, two things were true: (1) the situations resulted from uncontrollable circumstances of nature and/or the actions of people, not the actions of God; (2) God was utterly present in the moment, and the possibility of transformation was always available.

Our study pointed clearly to the reality that **God is available in every moment, but not causal to the moment.** It is an incredibly important distinction.

Just as it is possible for us to shut God out of the conscious consideration of our life, it is also possible for us to perform actions which are destructive in our life and in the lives of others. We cannot hold God responsible for *our* actions. The remarkable thing is that there is a dimension of life which breaks through the worst that can happen or that we can do and transforms it in ways beyond our imagining. There is no situation in which this possibility does not exist.

When we raise the question, "How can God allow this terrible thing to happen?" we have limited the presence and action of the Creative Mystery of the Universe to one situation and tried to blame this mystery (God) for not controlling the world in the way *we* know is right or the way *we* want it to be or think it ought to be.

None of the participants in our study ever asked that question. The question could have surfaced in many of the stories. In fact, the reality of God's presence transcended all other considerations.

Amazingly, the critical spiritual question, "Where is God in this moment?" makes all of this concern irrelevant. It allows us the possibility of letting go of the familiar, judgmental blindness that runs our lives and allows us to re-look at the world through the spiritual eyes of transformation which is always life changing. We are freed from our standard material assessments and now live in the simple, unfathomable place which our spirit recognizes as home.

That is the place where "Taking a Chance on God" is born and living in the moment with God becomes a reality.

10

Taking A Chance On God

In the thirteen years since we began our spiritual odyssey, we have become convinced that God is omnipresent: all the time, everywhere, in every situation and in every moment for every person. We are also aware that there are many impediments to experiencing this presence of God in our material world which is one of the reasons we wrote this book. We feel certain that God is here right now. But that does not mean that people are necessarily aware of this presence or know how to look for the signs that God is here. We are so imprisoned in our own egos that it is difficult to see anything that is not a product of us.

We know that God's presence in our lives carries with it the seeds of transformation and new life. We are free to recognize that presence or disregard or ignore it. We've discovered that recognizing God in our lives lays a claim on us to share that recognition with others and take some action in relation to the gift of God present with us. How, where or when that action takes place is up to the individual. But in spiritual terms, to not use the gift is to lose it.

We know that sharing stories about the presence or action of God with another person is a healing experience for both people. Within a group setting, this sharing becomes a potential healing experience for the entire group. When people begin a task by sharing their God stories, a new kind of group process occurs which is different from the normal group processes of which we are all familiar. This new group process begins with shared experiences of God as the focus of the group and moves from that commonality of experience to a different kind of connection in which we are united rather than divided.

We have seen in interfaith settings that such experiences are entirely different from the usual interfaith meetings in which differences are explained and some attempt made to reconcile them. As people share their God stories in this setting, similarities are immediately apparent which tends to create a marvelous unity of Spirit.

We live in a predominantly material world which has a powerful claim on us because it is our *default* position. Our data show there is another "world", the world of God present in each moment. When we choose to live our lives with God at the center, we have automatically reduced the maze of possibilities to one single focus: God. Now we have the possibility of opening our spiritual eyes and seeing any situation from a qualitatively different perspective and, for a moment, all other options retreat to the perimeter.

You can't see, hear or touch God, But God can touch your life in some wondrous and mysterious way which we can know but never explain.

So now we are faced with one more Mystery in our attempt to reach a place of closure in the telling of our story through the pages of this book.

We cannot provide you with a tidy plan or easily achieved goal with the steps to reach it. We cannot offer you the simplicity of a program which will help you reach some kind of spiritual result. We can't offer you money back guarantees, refunds or exchanges.

However, we can speak to you with the voices of people everywhere who have generously provided us with their words and stories about the presence and action of God in their lives. We can also tell you, with heart and passion, that as God has transformed our lives and the lives of so many in our study, we believe that God is just waiting for you to take the first step in acknowledging God in your life as well.

The strategy to do that is quite simple: **Take a Chance on God.** Assume God is right here, right now. We know that taking a chance on God is the most reliable, consistent and life giving message we can give you. And three thousand others would agree whole heartedly!

What does it mean to Take a Chance on God?" Well here are our suggestions, based on what we learned from our wonderful sample and what we know from our own lives.

You might call it our "non-program-program":

-Take thirty days and decide that you will try to look at your life experiences as containing the gift of the presence or action of God in that period of time.

-Assume that God is present and active in every moment.

-Act as if this were true and see what happens.

-Look for your story when God became *real* to you and use it to anchor you in a new "default" position.

-If a story doesn't come to you immediately, keep looking.

-Don't look for God in the usual places.

-Entertain the possibility that God is right here, right now.

-Try to shape your thinking to what you have read in this book. Remember! We have a remarkable ability to create our own reality. That is the quantum effect in which our measurement creates the reality it seeks to measure. Only this time, you are giving yourself over to the original Creator whose measurement can transform your life.

-If you started a notebook of words and stories, retrieve it and begin a new page called: "Living in the Moment with God".

-List those moments you've experienced when God might just have been around. The fact that you single out these moments is probably an indicator that God was right there.

-Run a parallel test. Explain those same experiences in the usual social/psychological material way. Then try to explain them as gifts from God.

-Note the differences between them.

-Don't automatically reject far out or unusual notions that may be part of this identification process. God is not limited by the way *we* organize our lives.

-Remember God gives spiritual gifts. Do not try to turn them into material gifts.

-Don't forget that God's other name, surprise, allows for a much broader picture of our spiritual lives. What may seem odd or peculiar to us may make great spiritual sense.

-We are remarkably self absorbed creatures. Although God is present all the time, we usually consider God most present when we are presented with problems and want God to fix them or make them go away.

-Concentrate instead on the idea that even problems contain a gift waiting for us to open. This is the UPS or FedEx model of God. Look at the problem as a package which has a meaning other than whatever the problem seems to be. Don't look for a solution, look for a meaning.

-Pray, but not for a solution, but for help in opening the gift.

-Give it a little time to incubate. It takes time to unwrap a gift. But tuck into the back of your mind that God is concerned with loving you and this problem may be the present doorway of God's concern.

-Share your story any time with anyone who will listen.

-If a plan of action occurs to you, consider that this may be an expression of God acting in the world through you. Don't lose the opportunity to act on this gift.

-Know that you can be vulnerable to God for, unlike the world of people, God will only love you in ways far beyond your ability to comprehend.

-The problem is not *will* we receive God's Gift, but will be able to cope with God's generosity.

-So, go with it.

-Stay open to what you discover.

-Stop trying to control the outcome.

-Do not make these suggestions into a program for achieving anything.

   -There are no ten or any other number of steps in this arena.

   -Be prepared for a surprise!

   -Again, stop trying to control the outcome.

   -Take a chance that

GOD IS HERE;
GOD IS REAL;
GOD IS NOW.

THE END?
NO,
JUST THE BEGINNING!

PART III
Appendix

Appendix

A. A Surprising New Look At Spirituality In The Mainstream

We've covered a lot of ground since we began this project. Thirteen years ago we were advised that no one was interested in the subject of Spiritual Healing in the United Church of Christ. Clearly our advisors were mistaken.

In selecting a sample for our study, we chose religious populations in the mainstream because we knew that other more Evangelical or Fundamentalist congregations already had a language and a venue in which to describe spiritual healing. We were looking for a population that reflected the average, mainstream religious understanding of the meaning of Spiritual Healing.

What we found was an "invisible" congregation within congregations who had profound experiences of the Presence or Action of God in their lives. What's more, this was not limited to Protestants. Our study was replicated in mainstream Catholic as well as Reform Jewish Congregations.

Everywhere we went across the United States we found this invisible spiritual community. What made these people invisible was that they simply didn't talk about their experience(s), even in their religious community.

Our study found an aspect of our religious culture that goes largely unnoticed, but which we discovered was very much alive, active and available. Given a supportive venue for sharing stories about the presence of God in their lives, people in our study were eager to show us just how active God is in everyday life.

People have experiences of the presence or action of God outside of membership in religious institutions. In fact, the Gallup Organization found "that 4 in 10 Americans have had a religious or spiritual experience that changed their lives." (George Gallup, Spirituality at Work Online Conference, 2003). Our study was restricted to religious congregations in the mainstream and did not pursue the question outside of these institutions.

The common perception is that spiritual healing experiences are thought to exist either in the Religious Right or in New Age Spirituality and not part of the main stream view or vocabulary of spiritual life. The idea that spiritual experience is the province of the religious right or new age secularism is certainly challenged by our findings. In fact, the assumption that America is becoming a secular society is a questionable assumption at best, based on our research.

We find this to be very exciting and not at all surprising. After all, we're talking about God, the Creative Mystery of the Universe. And God is not about to be confined by any of society's restrictions or ideas!

B. About Our Study

The Spiritual Healing Project is a study based on the collection of words and stories of the meaning of spiritual healing in the lives of people in mainstream Protestant, Catholic and Reform Jewish Congregations. It includes a nine page questionnaire written specifically for this study.

The original sample of one hundred churches in the United Church of Christ was based on a randomized sample which included ethnic, socioeconomic, preference and geographic diversity. The Catholic sample was designed to match the ethnic and socioeconomic diversity of the original sample within the Catholic Archdiocese of Chicago. The Reform Jewish sample was located in the Chicago Suburban area, as well as downstate Illinois and Wisconsin. The Episcopal sample was selected from churches in the Chicago and suburban areas and also reflected ethnic and socioeconomic diversity.

All the words and stories were collected in a group setting. The nine page questionnaires were also completed at the end of the group session. No information about spiritual healing was given nor were there any indications that spiritual healing (undefined) would take place in these sessions. These were clearly data gathering sessions. The researchers did not do a review of the literature on spiritual healing nor did they form hypotheses having to do with the subject. All of the above was explained to the sample before the data were collected.

The participants were asked to share words or phrases they associated to the words "spiritual healing". These words or phrases were catalogued alphabetically later and a frequency analysis was done. The participants were then asked to share stories of spiritual healing according to their own understanding of the subject, whether these were stories from their own lives or from the lives of others.

These stories were taken down verbatim and later transcribed into a computer file. The quantitative material from the questionnaires were data processed at the Center for Learning and Health, Department of Psychiatry and Behavioral Sciences, Johns Hopkins University School of Medicine. An analysis of the quantitative data was completed at the University of Pennsylvania.

As in all studies of human behavior, one must recognize the limitations as well as the pervasiveness of the results. Not all of the questions were answered by every participant. The responses we have shown are the responses of the participants and are not project-able to a larger population. In spite of the unusually large number and diversity of participants in this study, we are aware that our study was conducted in certain religious settings and not in all religious organizations. We did not conduct our research outside of religious institutions. Our Judeo-Christian sample did not include people from other religious affiliations.

However, our connection with the Alistar Hardy Religious Experience Research Centre assisted in bringing us stories from other world religions which provided a basis of comparison. The unfolding similarity of story themes gathered from our sample and the stories we read at the Alistar Hardy Research Centre certainly points the way toward a universal language of healing that supersedes and potentially transcends our avowed religious differences.

We have reported on the content of the stories, the data from the questionnaires and our experience in collecting these data. Our five observations were developed from our data and are a reflection of what the stories had to tell us in conjunction with the data analysis.

C. All The Shared Words From The Study

Spiritual Healing is:

Acceptance, awe, affirmation, answers, assurance, abundance, awareness, aligned, anticipation, atonement, at-one-ment, authentic, alleluia! (being) awake, accepting what you hadn't planned; accepting what you didn't want to happen.

Belief, blessing, balance, beauty, breath, bonding, birthing, buoyancy, beginning, being different, bliss! being called by name; being held in God's arms; becoming an insider; being put where you need to be; being at home in the moment; being on cruise control with God keeping the speed!

Comfort, connectedness, community, cleansing, creativity, courage, completeness, clarity, compassion, caring, contentment, Christ, conversion, centered, calm, change, Christian Science, charismatic, clearing out, cost, confession, commitment, confidence, closure, coming home; change of state: you feel better; continually being thrown on a potter's wheel with parts being stripped away and changing; cultivating an attitude of gratitude.

Discipline, discovery, deliverance, devotion, delicious, distinct, yet universal; direction out of the wilderness; despair is the movement of the soul toward healing; (like) dolphins following in God's wake.

Energy, empowerment, encircled, encompassing, endurance, excitement, elation, empathy, evangelism, ecstasy, eternal, enlightenment, ego-less, exhileration; encircled in God's love; everything in life is spiritual healing; (an) elusive moment of exquisite beauty.

Faith, forgiveness, freedom, filled, fulfillment, fearless, finding, flexibility, flame; finding something that is broken; feeling grounded in the world, yet liberated from it; finding the Holy in the ordinary!

Grace, gratitude, growth, giving, guidance, generative, gift, giving up the outcome; God's ministry to us.

Hope, healing, Holy spirit, humility, harmony, honesty, heaven, helping, happiness, Holy! healing the patient doesn't mean curing the disease; healing is done by God, not us.

Integration, inspiration, immediacy, indebtedness, invoking, insight! intense awareness of being loved by God; insanity is doing the same thing, in the same way, and expecting different results! spiritual healing breaks the cycle, immunization from past mistakes.

Joy, journey, Jesus! (a) journey to the very core of ourselves where God resides, just like love: you have to give it away to receive it.

Knowledge, kneeling, (the) knowledge that healing takes place *is* the great gift.

Love, letting go, learning, listening, laughter, lightness, liberation! like a caterpillar, we end up wrapped in our own little cocoon. then we break out as a butterfly, (a) lifelong dance of learning and practicing.

Mystery, miracle, meditation, mindfulness, mercy, mission, meaning, movement, maturing, melting, mending, mind/body connection, music! more of thee and less of me; (a) moment of the awareness when I say "yes!" (the) mystery of the Mystery!

Newness, new life, new beginning, new directions, nurture! (the) natural state of our relationship with God; never complete—always in process.

Openness, obedience, oneness, opportunity, ordinary, ongoing, optimistic, overcoming, out of control, outrageous joy! (being) open to the irrational and the unexpected opportunity, once received, you have an obligation to do something, to take action!

Peace, prayer, process, powerful, patience, possibility, paradox, positive thinking, purpose, presence, perspective, persistence, pain, progress, pristine, purging, promise, partnership with God; (a) paradigm shift; profound love; (the) possible of God in the midst of our impossible.

Quiet! (learning to be) quiet and listen.

Reconciliation, release, relief, renewal, resurrection, recovery, reunion, reassurance, redemption, risk, return, reverence, respect, repent, revealed, relinquish, relationship, restless, remembering, receive, resolution, rediscovery, reawakening, remission, recycling, recreation, resurrendering, rededication, retrospective, reborn! respect God's timing: God is never late! (the) restoring of the soul. reawakening of the known but forgotten; radical dependency.

Surrender, surprise, submission, serenity, strength, sharing, seeking, service, support, salvation, sureness, silence, solitude, synchronicity, searching, simplify, safety, security, sincerity, struggle, shift, soul, soul mending, soul-va-tion, sunshine! spiritual healing is a life preserver; spiritual healing breaks the crust; spiritual healing is a second chance.

Trust, transformation, touch, thanksgiving, tears, truth, transcendent, time, transfigured, trans-rational, transmutation, together, topsy-turvy! there is a divine structure in the ugly moments of life that needs to be discovered; the surround of God's love.

Understanding, unplanned, unexpected, unconditional, uplifting, unlimited, unearned, unafraid, unselfish, unlearning, unity! (being) used by God; unexpected joy!

Victory, vitality, vulnerable, vortex! (God's) vision of who we are as opposed to who we think we are. (a) verb victory over victimization!

Wholeness, work, (hard) work, warmth, wisdom, waiting, willingness, wonder, wonderful, witnessing, wounded, weaving together, weeping, wow! (a) wake up call; (i am) willing, please make me able; what other kind of healing is there?

Yes, yoke, yahoo! (if) you pray for something specific and you don't get an answer, that *is* the answer.

D. The Abc's Of Building A Spiritual Portfolio

Assume that God is present and active in the world all the time.

Build your spiritual portfolio as faithfully as your financial one.

Create a plan and try it for 30 days.

Don't be afraid.

Entertain the possibility that God is right here, right now.

Feeling good is not a requirement.

Get ready to be surprised by God.

Happy ever after is not the point.

Invest in God first.

Jump in: the water of God is wonderful.

Keep your spiritual eyes open at all times.

Look for your own story of God in your life: let it be your spiritual life-line.

Make a promise to yourself to ask, "Where is God?" in all situations.

Not everyone will like the transformed you.

Open your heart to the Spirit of God everywhere.

Prepare yourself to be transformed.

Questions, questions, questions—not answers.

Remember: You will forget and need to be reminded of God's presence in your life.

Share stories of God whenever and wherever possible.

Talk about God with anyone who will listen.

Understand that we don't control anything.

View your life with spiritual eyes.

When in doubt, stop, look and listen for God.

X out your ego whenever possible.

You can always begin again and again and again.

Zero in on the most important question you will ever ask: "Where is God in this moment?" And the answer is always: Right here! Right now!

E. Our Five Observations

1. God is present and active in the world.

2. This activity of God is a statistical reality and not a matter of faith alone.

3. There is a dimension to our lives that is legitimately called "spiritual" and which differs qualitatively from the material and has the power to transform it.

4. Transformation begins with the acknowledgment of the presence of God in the moment.

5. Having received the gift of God's presence in our lives, we have an obligation to share it.

F. Some of the Responses to our Questions: Percentages reflect the responses given.

What is Your Age? What is Your Gender?

Overall

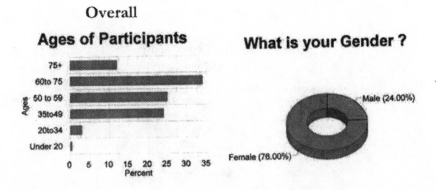

Ages of Participants

What is your Gender ?

Ages of Participants by Religion

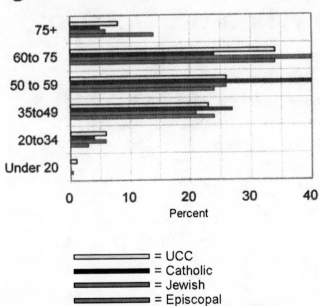

If you have experienced "spiritual healing", at what age did this happen to you?

Please check all responses that apply.

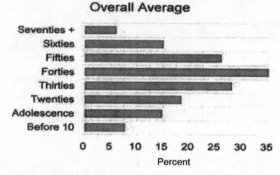

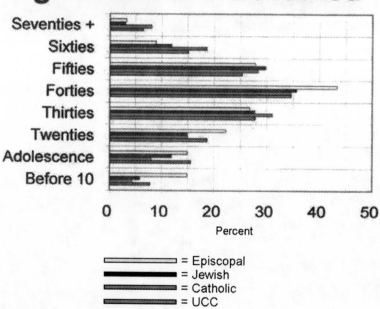

Has your understanding of who you are (your self identity) changed since your experience of spiritual healing?

	Yes
UCC	83%
Catholic	88%
Jewish	78%
Episcopal	76%

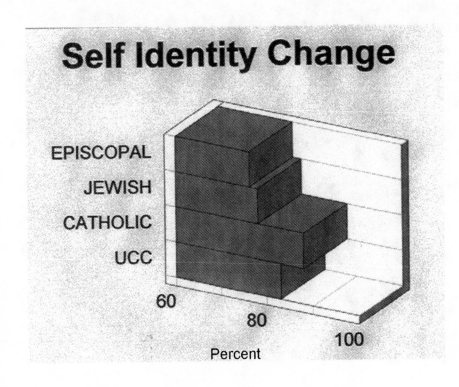

Self Identity Change
Overall Average

No (16.36%)

Yes (83.64%)

Self Identity Change

Generally speaking, has your life changed as a result of your spiritual healing?

	Yes
UCC	90%
Catholic	94%
Jewish	85%
Episcopal	85%

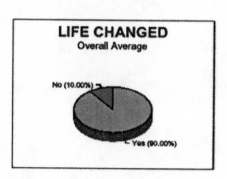

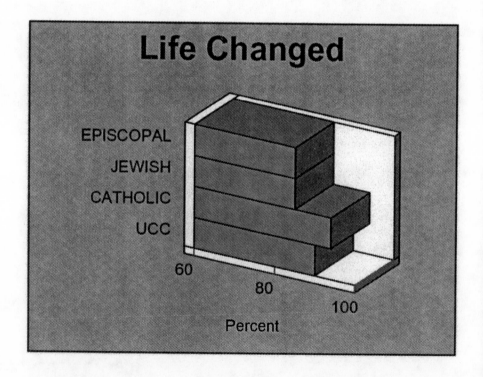

Age When SH Occurred
Overall Average

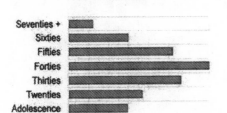

The ages most associated with Spiritual Healing are between 30 - 59 with a drop off from 60 on.

Our sample of participants was weighted toward the older side of the age range.

Ages of Participants

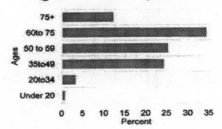

The combined data show most clearly the relationship between Church/Temple attendance, age of the Spiritual Healing experience and the age of the participants

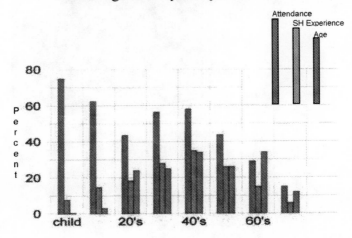

Did you feel a sense of surrender in your healing experience?

	Yes
Jewish	70%
Episcopal	96%
Catholic	95%
UCC	92%

Overall

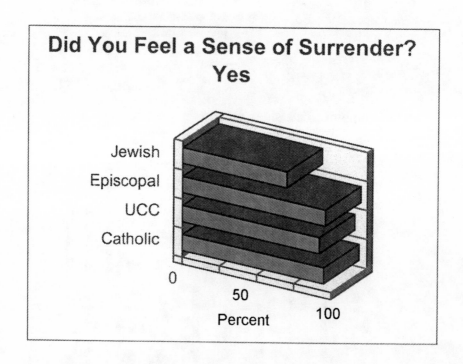

No (9.00%)

Yes (91.00%)

Did You Feel a Sense of Surrender?
Yes

Jewish
Episcopal
UCC
Catholic

0

50

100

Percent

What kind of support systems do you have?

Please check all that apply.

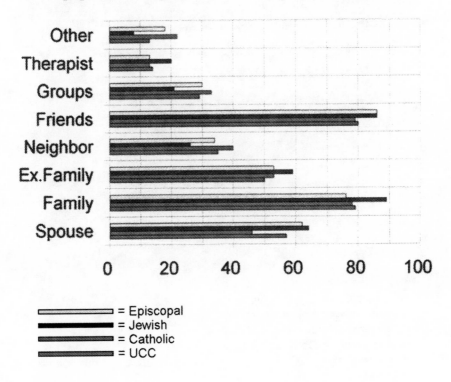

Support Systems by Religion

* The "Ex.Family" as shown in the diagram — means Extended Family.

What is your educational background?

Please check all that apply.

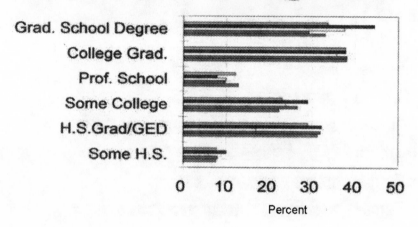

Educational Background

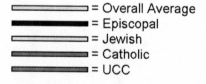
= Overall Average
= Episcopal
= Jewish
= Catholic
= UCC

Interactions of Pastor & Members

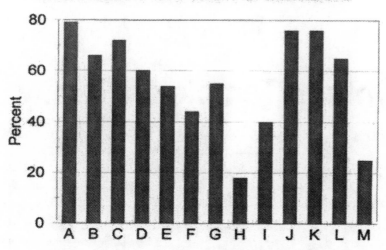

Have any of the following interactions between you and your pastor(s) and other church members helped you to feel some aspect of healing?

Check as many as apply.

A:	Listening to me	79%
B:	Telling me of <u>their</u> experiences	66%
C:	Praying with me	72%
D:	Telephoning me to see how I am	60%
E:	Inviting me to an activity at church	54%
F:	Inviting me to an activity outside of church	44%
G:	Helping me or my family in an emergency	55%
H:	Bringing me communion at home/hospital	18%
I:	Visiting me in hospital	40%
J:	Giving me a hug	76%
K:	Being interested in who I am	76%
L:	Sharing their problems with me	65%
M:	Other	25%

To what extent does this church/temple serve as a family for you?

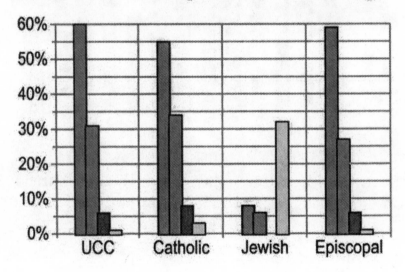

Church/Temple as Family

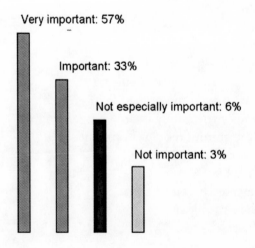

Very important: 57%

Important: 33%

Not especially important: 6%

Not important: 3%

Author's Credentials

Reverend Bobbie McKay, Ph.D., is a graduate of Garrett Theological Seminary who also holds a Ph.D. in Counseling Psychology from Northwestern University. She is a licensed clinical psychologist and an ordained minister in the United Church of Christ. Dr. McKay has been engaged in both of these helping/healing professions for over thirty years. She is the author of two books published by Pilgrim Press: *"The Unabridged Woman: A Guide to Growing Up Female"* and *"Whatever Happened to the Family: A Psychologist Looks at Sixty Years of Change,"* as well as numerous articles about children, families, marriage and spiritual growth. She has led over 900 seminars and workshops having to do with spiritual and psychological health and appeared on both television and radio. She has also worked extensively with Clergy pain, stress and burnout.

Lewis A. Musil, MFA, holds a Bachelors Degree from the University of Chicago and a Master of Fine Arts Degree from the Art Institute, Chicago, Illinois. Mr. Musil was a writer, producer and director of theater and television for twenty years. He was awarded a grant from the Field Foundation for an innovative theater project on Chicago's west side. He has taught extensively. He was a Visiting Professor in the use of Religion and the Arts at Garrett Theological Seminary for two years. He also taught at Elmhurst College and the Goodman Theater School of the Art Institute. He was Chairman of the Department of Creative Drama in the Evanston Public Schools for sixteen years.

Since 1994, both Dr. McKay and Mr. Musil have been involved in three research projects: The Spiritual Healing Project, an original, international study on the meaning of Spiritual Healing for people in mainstream religious communities; The Spiritual

Aging Project, a study of spirituality in the aging process; and The Spiritual Health Project, a study of the meaning of spiritual health.

Dr. McKay and Mr. Musil have already published "Healing the Spirit: Stories of Transformation," Thomas More Press, 2000. Their research appears in "Religion and Healing in America," Oxford University Press, 2005 (Chapter 2).

Dr. McKay and Mr. Musil are also adjunct faculty at Chicago Theological Seminary.

You can reach Dr. McKay and Mr. Musil at their web site: **www.spiritualhealthcenter.org**

978-0-595-46097-7
0-595-46097-6

Printed in the United States
125914LV00002B/18/A